TEACHING CHILDREN GAMES

Becoming a Master Teacher

DAVID E. BELKA, PhD
Miami University
Oxford, Ohio

Human Kinetics

28677081

Library of Congress Cataloging-in-Publication

Belka, David E., 1941-
    Teaching children games : becoming a master teacher / David E.
Belka.
        p.   cm.
    ISBN 087322-481-7
    1. Physical education for children--Study and teaching
(Elementary)--United States.   2. Games--Study and teaching
(Elementary)--United States.   3. Sports for children--United States.
I. Title.
GV221.B45   1994
372.86'0973--dc20   93-30702
                                                            CIP

ISBN: 0-87322-481-7

Acquisitions Editor: Scott Wikgren
AMTP Content Editor: Christine Hopple
Series Editor: George Graham, PhD
Developmental Editor: Julia Anderson
Assistant Editors: Sally Bayless and Anna Curry
Copyeditor: Jane Bowers
Proofreader: Kathy Bennett
Production Director: Ernie Noa
Typesetting and Text Layout: Sandra Meier
Illustration Coordinators: Tara Welsch and Kris Ding
Text Designer: Keith Blomberg
Cover Designer: Jody Boles
Photographer (cover): Bob Veltri
Illustrators: Mary Yemma Long, Kathy Boudreau-Fuoss, and Gretchen Walters
Printer: United Graphics
Cover Models: Andrew Baffi, Nick Baffi, Emily Carstenson, and Jennifer Shephard

Printed in the United States of America

10   9   8   7   6   5   4   3

Human Kinetics
Web site: http://www.humankinetics.com/

United States: Human Kinetics, P.O. Box 5076, Champaign, IL 61825-5076
1-800-747-4457
e-mail: humank@hkusa.com

Canada: Human Kinetics, Box 24040, Windsor, ON N8Y 4Y9
1-800-465-7301 (in Canada only)
e-mail: humank@hkcanada.com

Europe: Human Kinetics, P.O. Box IW14, Leeds LS16 6TR, United Kingdom
(44) 1132 781708
e-mail: humank@hkeurope.com

Australia: Human Kinetics, 57A Price Avenue, Lower Mitcham, South Australia 5062
(08) 277 1555
e-mail: humank@hkaustralia.com

New Zealand: Human Kinetics, P.O. Box 105-231, Auckland 1
(09) 523 3462
e-mail: humank@hknewz.com

Contents

Series Preface

In the United States most children spend 6 to 7 years in elementary schools, from kindergarten through sixth grade. Assume that they participate in instructional physical education classes twice a week for the entire time. Each class is 30 minutes long—a total of 36 hours a year and 216 hours over 6 years. Because of interruptions such as snow days, field trips, school plays, absences, and arriving late to physical education class, the time actually spent in physical education may be closer to 150 hours—perhaps less. Still 150 hours is a substantial amount of time. But what do children learn in that time? What is realistic to expect they might learn?

The answers vary. Some children might learn that physical activity is enjoyable, something they choose to do on their own with friends after school and on weekends. Others might learn that they are not good at sports and search for other ways to spend their leisure time. Others might really like their PE classes and the teacher but, given a choice, prefer to watch television or sit around when they're at home. The 150 hours, hopefully more, that a child spends in physical education classes influence his or her decisions— as a child, and for a lifetime!

What do we expect children to learn in elementary school physical education? Until recently the answer to this question was left solely to the individual teacher or school district. Physical educators across the United States had no universal sense of the outcomes that might accrue from quality programs of physical education. But this changed in 1992, when the National Association for Sport and Physical Education (NASPE) completed 7 years of work on a document titled *The Physically Educated Person*. This document outlined, for the first time, a nationally developed and endorsed framework for planning and evaluating physical education programs, from preschool through Grade 12. This book, and the other volumes in this series, was developed using the outcomes and benchmarks developed by NASPE as a general guide.

As you might imagine, the American Master Teacher Program (AMTP) struggled with how to organize the content. Should there be one book? Several books? Which model should we use to organize the content? Ultimately we chose to develop five books on the following topics: basic movement skills and concepts, games, gymnastics, dance, and fitness concepts. We decided to publish several books instead of just one because it seemed to be the most widely understood approach to organizing the content in physical education. It also provided the opportunity to involve several authors who were recognized for their expertise in their respective areas.

As we were considering possible authors, we made lists of who we thought were the best qualified individuals to write these books. In each instance, we are delighted to say, the author or authors we thought most qualified accepted our invitation to write the book. The books are as follows:

- *Teaching Children Movement Concepts and Skills: Becoming a Master Teacher* by Craig Buschner
- *Teaching Children Dance: Becoming a Master Teacher* by Theresa Purcell
- *Teaching Children Gymnastics: Becoming a Master Teacher* by Peter Werner
- *Teaching Children Games: Becoming a Master Teacher* by David Belka
- *Teaching Children Fitness: Becoming a Master Teacher* by Tom and Laraine Ratliffe

In addition, we want to thank Dr. Paula Ely, principal of Margaret Beeks Elementary School in Blacksburg, VA, for her ongoing support of various aspects of the American Master Teacher Program.

Each book is divided into two parts. The first part contains five chapters, which include a description of the content, an explanation of how it is organized, and most importantly the reasons why the author or authors believe that content is important for children to learn. One problem that has plagued physical education in elementary schools is that programs all too often have lacked an underlying theory or purpose. It seemed that teachers were just trying to entertain the children, rather than to actually teach them. For this reason, we hope you will begin reading this book by carefully reading Part I so that you can better understand the content—and *why* it is important for children to learn.

Part II contains the activities, or learning experiences (LEs). Five chapters contain the actual "stuff" to do with children. It is more than just stuff, however. Part II presents a logical progression of activities designed to lead children toward a heightened understanding and improved competence in the content described in the book. After you read the content described in Part I, you will be better able to envision where the LEs are leading—and the importance of the progression and sequencing of these activities will be clear to you. From the standpoint of the author, and ultimately the children, it would be unfortunate if a teacher completely skipped Part I and then searched Part II for activities that appeared to be the most fun and exciting—and then taught them in a haphazard way without any logical sequencing or order to the program. Children truly enjoy learning! These books are designed to help them do just that; the purpose is not just to keep them busy for a few minutes several times a week.

Finally, it is important to emphasize that *the contents of all five books are important* for the children's physical education. One danger in doing a series of books is that a mistaken impression might be given that a content area can be skipped altogether. This is not the case. Just as it wouldn't make sense for math teachers to skip subtraction or division because they didn't like to "take things away" or "weren't very good at it," it doesn't make sense to skip dance or gymnastics, for example, because a teacher has never had a course in it or isn't confident about teaching it. We realize, however, that many physical education teachers feel less confident about teaching dance or gymnastics; this is the primary reason the books were written—and why the AMTP was founded. It is certainly OK to feel anxious or unconfident about teaching one, or more, of the content areas. It's not OK, however, not to teach them because of these feelings. Many of us have experienced these same feelings, but with experience, work, and support, we have gradually incorporated them into our programs—and done so in ways that are both beneficial and enjoyable for children. This is what we want to help you to do as well. And that's why the books were written and the AMTP was developed.

Each of the five content books also has a companion videotape that provides examples of actual lessons selected from the learning experiences. These consolidated lessons show you how a few LEs might be developed with children. In addition to the videotapes, workshops are available through the American Master Teacher Program to help you gain a better understanding of the content and how it is taught. The authors of the books realize that making the transition from a traditional program to teaching this content is not easy, and yet increasingly teachers are realizing that children deserve more than simply being entertained in the name of physical education. We hope you will find the books worthwhile—and helpful—and that the children you teach will benefit!

George Graham
Cofounder and Director of Curriculum
    and Instruction
American Master Teacher Program

Preface

As I visit schools and work with prospective and practicing teachers, I find great disparity among teachers in their thinking about what games are and what games can do for children. Sometimes I see such contrast between skill work and game play. Other times I observe incongruency between tasks in the same lesson. Often the main emphasis is on learning rules, not playing to become a better player. What a teacher says are game values sometimes differs from what he or she actually teaches. I see these differences among undergraduate physical education majors, beginning teachers, and experienced teachers. Sometimes I see some of these differences in my own teaching. Understanding and teaching games is not nearly as simple as it looks.

The purposes of this book are to (a) analyze how games are taught and provide a rationale for including games in the elementary physical education curriculum; (b) explain a framework and conceptual basis for teaching games to elementary children; and (c) present selected extended examples of games content. With so much written about games and the thousands of games in print, a rationale is essential to weed out the bad games and to select or design good games.

The first purpose will aid us in applying ideas about what needs to be in games instruction in the 1990s. Games must have beneficial educational outcomes, or they are being used only because they are fun for children. The second purpose is more difficult to understand and to write about. Missing in the past was a method or model to guide games teaching and to determine progression in games from simpler to more complex. A concept of games and even a structure are essential if games instruction is to improve. Extended examples of games content, the third purpose, make sense only in relation to the first two purposes.

Many children love games, no matter what kind they play. Other children are turned off by some games, by the way many games are dominated by a few children, and by the way teachers organize and conduct games. Part of this dislike may be because often games instruction provides little emphasis on learning usable strategies, few chances for everyone to practice skills or strategy, and little cognitive understanding of the games played. This book presents ideas that are designed to help alleviate each of these concerns.

In making decisions about what content to include in the elementary curriculum and what content to discard, teachers should consider recent ideas about teaching games. These include Rink's (1985, 1992) ideas for sequencing content and the recent position statements from committees of the American Alliance of Health, Physical Education, Recreation and Dance (Council on Physical Education for Children, 1992; Franck et al., 1991). Developmental perspectives need to be the bases for content progressions. It is time to make decisions about which content has the most worth, which has significant worth, which has less worth, and which has limited or no worth in the curriculum. Content chosen as significant and vital must have conceptual and curricular worth, as well as being sound developmentally.

This book is designed to be used with *Teaching Elementary Physical Education: Becoming a Master Teacher*, written by George Graham (1992). Graham's book is an overview of teaching elementary physical education. This games book is one of five dealing with content in elementary physical education. The other four books focus on fitness, dance, gymnastics, and motor skills and movement concepts.

There are 10 chapters in *Teaching Children Games*, divided into two parts. Part I, chapters 1 through 5, provides an analysis of games, a rationale and model for games instruction, and assessment ideas. These chapters focus on purposes of games, sequencing strategy instruction, special considerations in different teaching situations, types of games, criteria for selecting and developing games instruction, and evaluation of children's game play. Part II, chapters 6 through 10, presents numerous extended examples in the five categories of games plus program suggestions for implementation. For each game, prerequisites, objectives, equipment, and playing area are described. Each game is explained carefully, and ideas to make the games simpler or more difficult are included. The appendix presents lesson plan information; selected readings are suggested for additional reference.

I appreciate the encouragement I received from Scott Wikgren at Human Kinetics and editor George Graham. The professionalism and sensitivity shown by curriculum specialist Christine Hopple and developmental editor Julia Anderson helped me and motivated me immensely. Special thanks are extended to Sarah Doolittle for reviewing chapters and sharing ideas and game examples; Amy Mays Woods for extended idea discussions and motivation; Jim Batesky and Kathy Pottak for reviewing games and early drafts; Susan Lipnickey for listening for hours to revisions; Nancy Cross for game ideas; and my wife, Jan, for always being with me.

David Belka

Part I

Developmentally Appropriate Games

In 1992 the National Association for Sport and Physical Education (NASPE) published a document entitled *Developmentally Appropriate Physical Education Practices for Children*. The document, developed by the executive committee of the Council on Physical Education for Children (COPEC), represents the collective wisdom of many physical educators about what good elementary physical education is. The principles NASPE espoused in this document guided the development of this and the other four books in this series.

Part I begins with an overview of developmentally appropriate games, why they should be part of a quality elementary PE program, and how this approach differs from what has been traditionally taught in physical education. Chapter 1 also includes a definition of the physically educated person, including psychomotor, cognitive, and affective objectives, and a discussion of the significance of this definition for children's games instruction.

Virtually no two teaching situations are identical in physical education. Chapter 2 provides several suggestions on how you can structure your program to fit the idiosyncrasies of your school. Ideas for teaching lessons with limited space, equipment, and time are explained in this chapter. Quality programs can be developed in less-than-ideal situations, but it's not easy.

A complete description of the content, including definitions of terms specific to the content area, is provided in chapter 3. As you review the content of all five books, you will quickly see that they contain much more than fun games and activities that are designed simply to keep children occupied for 30 minutes or so. Each content area outlines a developmentally appropriate curriculum designed to provide children with a logical progression of tasks leading to skillfulness in, and enjoyment of, physical activity.

Chapter 4 describes and discusses the key teaching principles that are used to provide developmentally appropriate experiences for children. This chapter applies pedagogical principles as they relate specifically to teaching the content included in the book. As you know, each of the five content areas has unique characteristics that master teachers are aware of as they teach their lessons.

The final chapter in Part I is on assessment. It describes practical ways to assess how well children are learning the concepts and skills related to the content being taught. As we enter the 21st century, educators are increasingly being required to document, in realistic ways, the progress their children are making. This requirement presents unique challenges to the elementary school physical educator who may teach 600 or more children each week. Chapter 5 provides some realistic suggestions for ways to formatively assess what children are learning.

1

Why Is It Important to Teach Children Games?

What are games? This may seem like a simple question that does not need much explanation. But it does. Games, at least the way adults perceive and play them, typically involve controlling and manipulating an object. The object is usually a ball, but games also involve rackets, gloves, nets, pucks, goals, striking implements, and other kinds of equipment.

In *Teaching Children Games, games* are defined as activities that involve at least 2 people who often move about in a specified area. Usually an object is moved in certain ways; often other equipment is used. This definition excludes many activities that adults may label as games (board games, dominoes, darts, etc.) because these activities lack gross motor movement.

Games do not always need equipment. Games that involve running and dodging—such as tag—are part of many physical education programs, but games more often require skillful manipulation of an object. Prerequisite to such object manipulation, and necessary during games, is control of one's body. Gymnastics and dance help develop skill in locomotion and controlling one's body. Performers who can control their bodies well can focus attention on controlling an object during games play. Skills developed in gymnastics and dance transfer to games play. Fitness is necessary because endurance, flexibility, and aerobic and anaerobic power are needed in many games and aid performance in games.

Games are usually played according to rules, and strategy is important. Games involve many aspects (see Figure 1.1). The extent to which a game teaches skillful games playing and the extent to which it teaches strategic decision making are criteria that will be used to include some games and to exclude others. Learning strategy and applying skills one has learned are the basics of games instruction. Extended instruction in gamelike skills, such as throwing or kicking, is simply skill work and is gamelike, but it is not games instruction. Mirroring a partner, for example, or moving or dribbling to maintain a specified distance from a partner can be gamelike, but it is not a game. It is skill work, and very important skill work.

Criticisms of Traditional Games

Although games are generally accepted as valuable, more and more educators are questioning their place: Are games valuable for all children? Exactly what should the purposes of games be?

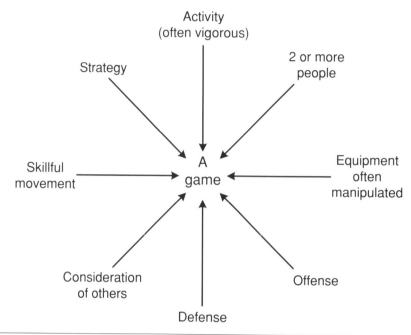

Figure 1.1   Games are comprised of many elements.

How can games be used to benefit all children? The traditional teaching of games has been criticized for a number of reasons, including these:

- It favors the highly skilled students (elitism).
- It is often used simply to expend students' excess energy or to provide an academic break.
- It does not specify learning outcomes; rather, the goal is just having fun.
- It neglects developmental principles.
- It uses a teacher-centered approach.
- Students spend much time standing, not learning.
- Games have weak learning progressions.

Games Favor the Highly Skilled

Games have been criticized as elitist, with highly skilled children dominating play disproportionately in scoring, time of possession of the object, and the amount and quality of positive feedback from the teacher. Races that end with a single winner, without instruction about improving form or speed, may promote superiority of a few and neglect performance instruction altogether. Elimination games are still being played in many PE classes; much of the time, the higher skilled dominate and the lesser skilled, who need the practice time, are eliminated from the game for

long periods. In large-group games, such as kickball (Wilson, 1976), several skilled players dominate while other players never get an opportunity to field or throw (see Figure 1.2). The criticism that a games curriculum is elitist is certainly one that all of us need to examine in our own programs.

Games Expend Surplus Energy as an Academic Break

Using games to divert children's attention from classroom subjects and use up surplus energy is a rationale with no sound, educational basis, but one that is still prevalent. One commonly hears comments from classroom teachers to physical educators like "Work them hard so they come back to my classroom ready to learn." But the protocols physical educators use are designed to create an atmosphere for learning and to facilitate maximum learning (Graham, 1992), not to provide an extra class period or a "break."

Games Offer Fun, Not Learning Outcomes

Many of the low-organized games popular today (circle games, line games, large-group games) have no worthwhile movement performance objective (or at least do not achieve the movement objective as well as other activities). In fact,

Figure 1.2   Do we need to use games that foster elitism?

many such games (such as Duck, Duck, Goose, Midnight, and Kickball) have been replaced by emphasis on movement performance that focuses on body awareness, space awareness, effort, and relationships (Council on Physical Education for Children, 1992; Buschner, 1994). Recent textbooks also reflect this change (Buschner, 1994; Graham, Holt/Hale, & Parker, 1993; Logsdon et al., 1984; Purcell, 1994; Rink, 1985; Werner, 1994).

Games should be enjoyable and fun, but the main rationale for them cannot be this alone. Students need to learn about manipulating objects, about using skills in more complex game situations, about trying out different strategies of game play, and about controlling objects to achieve higher levels of play. For example, games can teach students how to move without the ball to create open spaces, how to use fakes to confuse the defense, or how to stay between the offense and the goal and create problems for a dribbler. "They didn't learn much, but they had a great time" must become "They had fun and they really learned."

Games Overlook Developmental Principles

Traditional programs are not based on movement development principles. For example, Call Ball is a game in which 15 to 25 kindergarten children stand in a circle with 1 child in the center holding a ball. The child calls another's name and throws the ball into the air. The child called moves toward the ball and attempts to catch it. The easiest type of catch is when a softly arced ball arrives at body midline, probably sent from the same height as caught (Belka, 1985; Herkowitz, 1978; Morris, 1976, 1980). The children should be allowed adequate practice with this type of catch before doing the vertical catch. Also, stationary catching precedes moving to catch. But the teacher may not have used, or even considered, these developmental principles, when planning the low-organized game Call Ball. In team games, often the children are placed in situations that are too complex for them to succeed in unless they have had considerable experience in similar activities outside of physical education. And these experienced students need the practice the least.

Games Are Teacher-Centered

Many of the low-organized and lead-up games are teacher-centered. The teacher preplans the game, establishes and teaches the rules and organization, controls the pace, and often referees too. Sometimes the teacher referees and also pitches. In the classic example, one game is played, with 12 to 15 children on each side. Traditional games fail to allow for a child-centered approach, the approach that most elementary curriculum texts emphasize. Child-centered learning, in which the child makes decisions about his or her learning, occurs when teachers empower children to make decisions and to take responsibility for part of their learning (see Graham, 1992, pp. 128-138).

Games Emphasize Standing, Not Learning

With many low-organized and lead-up games, children spend considerable time waiting for turns. I have observed classes of 30 in which the game action was 3 against 3 while the other 24 students waited for turns, sat on the stage, or were semispectators behind a restraining line. And sideline basketball or soccer can also have 75% to 80% waiting time. There is no excuse for forcing children to spend up to 80% to 90% of PE time waiting. Each student gets few turns, which are often poor in quality and too few to enable real learning. This prevents children from achieving the automatic skill level required for success in strategy games. Waiting also causes low activity; games cannot contribute to aerobic endurance unless vigorous activity is maintained for an extended period of time.

In these large-group games, often considerable time is devoted to organizing the game, and there is much dead time (waiting time) between attempts. Children with less ability are only "on stage" when they bat or kick. And their weak performances may elicit negative comments from displeased teammates. In the field, these children can "hide" while the attention is on the performance of the more assertive, better skilled players. Much of this can go unnoticed by teachers. How these activities are organized and how they are conducted are probably more serious shortcomings of the traditional method of teaching games than is the actual games content. The need for high-activity time (Graham, 1992, pp. 70-72) is just as important for games play as for single and combination skill learning.

Games Have Weak Learning Progressions

The traditional games model has been criticized as providing "things to do" rather than a sequential plan for learning to move (Logsdon et al.,

1984). Although the traditional model appears logical in its progression, there is often no plan for sequencing instruction. For example, within the low-organized games, one game may be as good as any other. The hundreds of tag games are about the same: One or 2 people are It and try to tag others. Often the children in one line try to cross over past these taggers or advance toward the taggers and, on a signal, run to a safety line. The children receive no instruction about balance, dodging, changing direction quickly, or strategy.

Activities are listed one after the other, without any explanation of what skills preceded that game, exactly what this game progressed toward, or what came after that particular game. There is a complete lack of progression from low-organized games to lead-up games. Low-organized games such as tag and simple ball games are taught without any emphasis on understanding movement or strategy. Teachers assume that the running and dodging in low-organized tag games transfers to lead-up games. But this is doubtful unless instruction is given about the process or the strategy of running and dodging in games. The relationship between low-organized games and lead-up games is weak, and sometimes nonexistent.

Although there is progression between lead-up games and the official versions of the adult sport, often the jumps needed in organization and skills are immense. The jumps in progression make success unlikely except for the highly skilled children who dominate the game. Often the emphasis in lead-up games is on learning how to play within the rules, not on learning strategies and skills that transfer to the official sport. Official games frequently require skills and strategies that are too difficult for most children. Or the progression in skills and strategies is ignored in teaching of the lead-up games. The games are played, but most children do *not* learn to be better games players. The focus is on the game, *not* learning to play games.

Although the traditional model for teaching games has been criticized severely as inadequate, it has survived. There are ways to organize games instruction that avoid these criticisms. Games instruction *can* promote more acceptable and desirable learning outcomes, as I hope to show in this book. The rest of this chapter deals with aspects that support an instructional approach that is developmentally appropriate for children's physical education.

Benefits of Child-Appropriate Games

There is reason for optimism. The 1990s may be the time when children's games instruction becomes more appropriate for the children's developmental levels. After lengthy study by professional groups, two important documents have been written recently (Council on Physical Education for Children, 1992; Franck et al., 1991). These documents are being discussed by educators across the United States and may have a major national impact.

The Physically Educated Person

The National Association for Sport and Physical Education (NASPE) has defined the "Physically Educated Person" and listed outcomes of quality physical education in Grades K through 12 (Franck et al., 1991). These are shown in Figure 1.3.

The five categories of a physically educated person (*has* learned skills, *is* physically fit, *does* participate regularly, *knows* the implications and benefits, and *values* physical activity) and the 20 outcomes relate to learning in the three domains (psychomotor, cognitive, and affective)

A Physically Educated Person:

- **Has** learned skills necessary to perform a variety of physical activities:
    1. Moves using concepts of body awareness, space awareness, effort, and relationships
    2. Demonstrates competence in a variety of manipulative, locomotor, and nonlocomotor skills
    3. Demonstrates competence in combinations of manipulative, locomotor, and nonlocomotor skills performed individually and with others
    4. Demonstrates competence in many different forms of physical activity
    5. Demonstrates proficiency in a few forms of physical activity
    6. Has learned how to learn new skills

- **Is** Physically fit:
    7. Assesses, achieves, and maintains physical fitness
    8. Designs safe, personal fitness programs in accordance with principles of training and conditioning

- **Does** participate regularly in physical activity:
    9. Participates in health-enhancing physical activity at least three times a week
    10. Selects and regularly participates in lifetime physical activities

- **Knows** the implications of and the benefits from involvement in physical activities:
    11. Identifies the benefits, costs, and obligations associated with regular participation in physical activity
    12. Recognizes the risk and safety factors associated with regular participation in physical activity
    13. Applies concepts and principles to the development of motor skills
    14. Understands that wellness involves more than being physically fit
    15. Knows the rules, strategies, and appropriate behaviors for selected physical activities
    16. Recognizes that participation in physical activity can lead to multicultural and international understanding
    17. Understands that physical activity provides the opportunity for enjoyment, self-expression, and communication

- **Values** physical activity and its contribution to a healthful lifestyle:
    18. Appreciates the relationships with others that result from participation in physical activity
    19. Respects the role that regular physical activity plays in the pursuit of lifelong health and well-being
    20. Cherishes the feelings that result from regular participation in physical activity

Figure 1.3 Outcomes of quality physical education programs. *Note.* The "Physically Educated Person" document containing these outcomes and accompanying benchmarks (see Figure 1.4) can be obtained by contacting NASPE at 1900 Association Drive, Reston, VA 22091-1599 or by calling 1-800-321-0789.
From *Physical Education Outcomes: A Project of the National Association for Sport and Physical Education* by M. Franck, G. Graham, H. Lawson, T. Loughrey, R. Ritson, M. Sanborn, and V. Seefeldt (the Outcomes Committee of NASPE), 1991. Copyright 1991 by NASPE. Reprinted by permission of the National Association for Sport and Physical Education, Reston, VA.

and can be used to design and evaluate a developmentally appropriate program. Outcomes 3, 4, 5, 6, 13, 15, 17, and 18 have particular significance for games instruction. In addition, NASPE provides examples of the five indicators to be used as benchmarks or outcomes that, at various grade levels, indicate program quality. Although these are intended only as examples, not absolute standards, it is helpful to know which ones are relevant to games instruction (see Figure 1.4). These examples provide guidance for planning and conducting games teaching; they are the starting point for evaluating our programs.

Appropriate and Inappropriate Practices

The other major document is a policy statement by the Council on Physical Education for Children (COPEC, 1992). This paper tries to communicate which practices the council deems appropriate for children and which practices should be eliminated from elementary physical education programs. Nineteen separate practices are identified with examples of appropriate and inappropriate use of each one. Desirable practices include a balanced curriculum of concept and skill development, dance, gymnastics, fitness, and games; undesirable is a curriculum planned around the teacher's interests, such as primarily group games. Appropriate physical education includes teaching a functional understanding of movement concepts, developing competent skill performance, and building confidence in one's ability; inappropriate physical education focuses on a limited number of games in which the opportunity for individuals to develop skills and learn concepts is restricted.

In desirable practices all children are continuously active in meaningful activities that are based on how children grow and develop. Although this COPEC statement addresses many topics for an entire elementary program, there is a continual need to look at how programs can be designed to develop competent games players, to consider the feelings and affective development of children, and to be equitable.

As a result of participating in a quality physical education program, it is reasonable to expect that the student will be able to do the following:

Psychomotor Domain (Has, Is, Does)

While traveling, avoid or catch an individual or object (3-4, #1)
Throw a variety of objects demonstrating both accuracy and distance (5-6, #1)
Hand-dribble and foot-dribble while preventing an opponent from stealing the ball (5-6, #5)
Consistently throw and catch a ball while guarded by opponents (5-6, #7)
Design and play small-group games that involve cooperating with others to keep an object away from
    opponents (basic offensive and defensive strategy (5-6, #8)

Cognitive Domain (Knows)

Distinguish between compliance and noncompliance with game rules and fair play (3-4, #18)
Recognize fundamental components and strategies used in simple games and activities (3-4, #20)
Designs games . . . that are personally interesting (3-4, #26)
Recognize the role of games . . . in getting to know and understand others of like and different cultures
    (5-6, #19)
Detect, analyze, and correct errors in personal movement patterns (and game play) (5-6, #24)

Affective Domain (Values)

Appreciate differences and similarities in others' physical activity (3-4, #27)
Celebrate personal successes and achievements and those of others (3-4, #30)
Accept and respect the decisions made by game officials, whether they be students, teachers, or
    officials outside the school (5-6, #26)

Figure 1.4 Sample benchmarks relevant for games. The first number in parentheses following each benchmark relates to the grade level that benchmark can be found under in the NASPE document; the second number gives the specific benchmark for that grade level. These will be referenced to objectives for learning experiences in Part II of this text, when appropriate. See page 49 for further information.
Note. From *Physical Education Outcomes: A Project of the National Association for Sport and Physical Education* by M. Franck, G. Graham, H. Lawson, T. Loughrey, R. Ritson, M. Sanborn, and V. Seefeldt (the Outcomes Committee of NASPE), 1991. Copyright 1991 by NASPE. Adapted by permission of the National Association for Sport and Physical Education, Reston, VA.

Cognitive Aspects of Games

In my formal education, I learned to play a number of games, some fairly well. But I did not become an adept, cognitive player. I learned to play games within a structure given to me by teachers or coaches. I learned rules and regulations, not reasons for doing things, and not strategies. In wrestling, I learned isolated moves; never was I instructed about the concept of breaking down an opponent's balance if I were in the *up* position. Nor did I learn to use the opponent's weight against him. In team sports, I was never given a general strategy, only specific ways to pass, catch, or move.

We need to help children understand reasons for sports rules and regulations, not just to learn the rules and regulations. Understanding mechanical, conceptual, and strategic concepts is an important part of physical education; such understanding should help children move better and apply strategy better. The child's next step after understanding is to relate what the child does to what he or she knows about the skill or strategy. This extends to why a game is played the way it is and whether the game should be modified to be fairer or to better meet playing needs.

Ideas about games play in this book are based on children's learning strategies. The child must decide when to do something, choose which strategy to use, and make these decisions quicker and quicker. Like skills, strategies must be learned—beginning with the simple and progressing to the complex. Learning strategies is the main content in beginning games instruction.

Social Aspects of Games

We need to scrutinize the games and activities we choose for elementary children for the social and emotional effects they can have on children. Games can benefit or detract from the child's ability to interact with others and affect the child's evaluation of whether he or she is becoming more competent or less competent in games play. Although part of this is knowledge, much of this refers to values, as described in Figure 1.4.

All of us compare how we perform to how others perform. Psychologists call this social comparison. It is normal for children age 8 or so to socially compare themselves with each other. Doing this is a form of evaluation, and the process

helps a child become aware of capabilities and limitations. The process is often healthy and useful, but sometimes it gets out of hand and becomes more important than it should be. Exaggerated use of comparisons should be held in check. One of the NASPE outcomes is to celebrate personal successes and achievements and those of others. The teacher's task is to encourage these celebrations in ways that are expressive but not inconsiderate of others.

Games, like many other activities, can be used to reinforce desirable and acceptable behaviors. Teachers and children can say and do things that help children learn what behaviors are acceptable and what behaviors are less acceptable. As a role model, I want to encourage teammates when I play and avoid making negative comments when teammates perform below expectations (see Figure 1.5). I need to follow the game rules to show the children a good model. I need to accept teacher's and referee's decisions without complaining; this is particularly important and different from what children see on televised sports. Such instructor behavior is needed to reinforce acceptable social behavior. It is an extension of Graham's (1992) pinpointing.

Children need time to discuss situations and understand respect and concern for others. This is a difficult outcome to achieve in games, or just in general in schools. Children need to learn to be concerned about the safety of others, play to earn (not take) advantages within rules, avoid

Figure 1.5 Teammates should use encouraging comments.

others' space and any behavior that could injure others, control their emotions, and demonstrate interpersonal behaviors that are acceptable and helpful. Children need to understand how other people feel about their own performances in and contributions to games and how they feel when they perform well or not so well. If peers give accepting and encouraging comments (see Figure 1.5), game play may improve and enjoyment may increase.

Fairness in Games

If the teacher provides a positive role model, reinforces desirable behaviors, and emphasizes respect and concern for others, this should lead to games that are fair—or more fair.

When rules are given to children without any real explanation of why the rules were devised, misinterpretations can easily occur. In the past, teachers have explained the rules, but not the reasons *for* the rules. A benchmark for quality programs is that children distinguish between compliance and noncompliance with game rules and fair play (Figure 1.3) and act accordingly.

If children are involved in making rules, modifying rules, and understanding reasons for rules, fewer misinterpretations will occur. Today's children cannot be expected to blindly adhere to rules given to them. Games instruction provides an opportunity to help children question reasons for rules, modify rules to make them fair, and evaluate behaviors in terms of what is fair.

Developmentally appropriate games provide opportunities for many children to have many turns in small-group games. If given the chance to select their own groups, children often choose others of similar ability so that there is less variance and less dominance by 1 or 2 children. Also, children in self-selected groups are more tolerant of differing abilities and try to include all children in the games (Riley, 1975). Self-selected groups provide lower skilled students with more skill chances in less complex settings and more chances for success. Lower skilled children, as well as girls (who are often restricted in games, even when a girl is more skilled than the boys in her group), have more opportunities to learn skills and games and are not given fewer roles or support roles (Griffin, 1981). Children are not expected to just receive a pass and pass it back to the best player, who then shoots to score.

Confidence and Self-Esteem in Games

Children need to develop confidence in their movement abilities, enjoy moving, be able to realistically evaluate their abilities, and experience success in controlling their movements.

Success breeds success in children's movement. When successful, children tend to perform the skill in subsequent attempts with more effective force production (Roberton & Halverson, 1984, p. 124). This is such a simple concept that we may have failed to realize it. Many children may profess an "I can't" attitude mainly because they do not feel successful in a movement, don't have confidence, and do not want to risk further attempts.

To foster a special confidence for movement in a child, you must build the child's self-confidence concurrently with movement competence (Romance, 1985). Doing so helps the child learn fundamental movement skills (single skills and combination skills) and accumulate knowledge that the child can use to move more effectively or more efficiently. And the child learns in a self-testing and self-assuring way. "I can!" is the confidence goal, with "I can't . . . yet" (Graham, 1992, pp. 140-141) the intermediate confidence slogan.

Teaching that uses mainly large-group games, adult team games, overemphasis on specific skills, and extreme competition is not consistent with movement implications based on child growth and development. Only after they attain competency in the skills, along with confidence, are children ready for games involving group competition. To progress in games, children need confidence in their skills, confidence in their decision making, and confidence in their teacher and playing atmosphere.

Games Stages

Games instruction has traditionally lacked a sequential model for planning and implementing instruction. Judy Rink, with the help of Ruth Earls (1985), designed a four-stage, developmentally appropriate model for teaching games. The four stages are as follows:

Stage 1   Maintaining and improving single skills

Stage 2   Combining two or more skills into smooth sequences

Stage 3   Learning beginning offensive and defensive strategies

Stage 4   Playing games with complex rules and strategies in teams with specialized player roles

The first two stages involve learning and improving object manipulation skills. Stage 1 focuses on a *single* skill. Many preschoolers and primary children need this kind of skill practice (Buschner, 1994). Young and inexperienced learners are at Stage 1, but even professional athletes spend enormous time and energy on Stage 1 single skills.

Stage 2 *combines* skills but includes practice on perfecting these combinations and increasing speed and precision when possible. Versatility in less predictable (i.e., more open) environments is one objective. Partners vary the height, distance, direction, speed, and force to increase the difficulty for a partner or small group. Children help partners become more skillful receivers and senders by challenging them but keeping the object within the partner's skill level (i.e., not making them miss). Much of the primary and intermediate work with manipulation skills will be in Stage 2. Children and adults are often challenged in learning and improving performance in putting skills together. And these challenges can be self-motivating as the skills are refined for better performance and extended to increase in difficulty. Figure 1.6 illustrates Stages 1 and 2.

Stage 1—Single skills like jumping

Stage 2—Skill combinations like jumping to catch and throw in the air

Figure 1.6   Skill learning in Stage 1 and 2 games.

Stages 3 and 4 are most useful when children can execute combined skills to near-automatic performance *and* begin to understand strategy. Because they do not need to think intensely about how to do the skill, they are ready to focus attention on deciding when and how *to use* the skill (Rink, 1985, 1992). The focus is no longer on learning and performing the skills but on learning and using offensive and defensive strategies. Players must take in information, make decisions, and then execute skills in an extremely short time span. Stage 4 is regulation play, with the sport's intricate rules, and regulation play areas and equipment; Stage 4 often includes spectators. Complex rules, many players, differentiated player roles, and intricate strategies make Stage 4 game play difficult for most elementary school children. One should not jump from skill learning in Stages 1 and 2 to complex Stage 4 games. Stage 3 provides an introduction to beginning offensive and defensive game play. The examples in Figure 1.7 show differences in strategies between Stage 3 and Stage 4 games.

What Is Stage 3 Game Play?

Children need to learn strategy and game playing in much the same way they learned single and combination skills, by beginning with *simplex* (my coined word, used for emphasis) and moving to *complex* situations. At first, rules should be few, the strategies limited, and the groups small in number. In these less complex settings, children have time to make decisions about offensive and defensive situations. As skills improve, decision time is reduced, opponent's strength is increased, and decision options are increased.

Children need much practice perfecting single and combination skills before they can benefit from participating in competitive games. Doolittle (1992) uses very simple skills, instead of perfected manipulation skills, to shorten the time needed to learn game strategies. For example, a child holds and throws a beanbag at a defended hoop. Most or all of the child's attention can be focused on learning and using the emphasized game strategies because manipulating the beanbag is easy. If the performance skills are complex and require extensive attention, the player cannot also attend well to strategy. This is evident in many complex games.

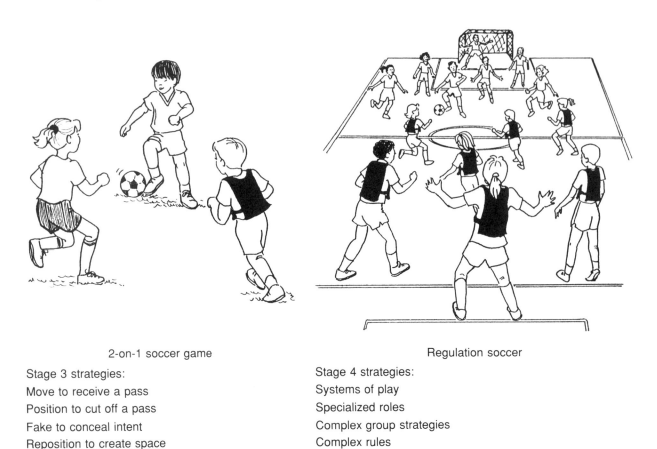

2-on-1 soccer game

Stage 3 strategies:

Move to receive a pass

Position to cut off a pass

Fake to conceal intent

Reposition to create space

Regulation soccer

Stage 4 strategies:

Systems of play

Specialized roles

Complex group strategies

Complex rules

Figure 1.7   Strategy learning in Stage 3 and 4 games.

Summary

Games, along with gymnastics and dance, are an important part of the content in elementary physical education programs. The traditional games program has serious content, organizational, and developmental problems. For their use to be justified in programs, games need clear, achievable, educational outcomes.

Games content needs to be congruent with recent national position statements published by NASPE and COPEC, both divisions of the American Alliance of Health, Physical Education, Recreation and Dance. Games need to relate to what a physically educated person is, does, has, knows, and values.

Achieving cognitive understanding, with an emphasis on strategy, is vital in learning to be a games player. Games need to be planned and organized carefully for social and emotional outcomes, too. Games must be developmentally appropriate to be justified. A model for organizing games so that they are sequenced and developmentally appropriate is available and constitutes the basis for teaching games in this book.

Chapter 2

Tailoring Games to Fit Your Teaching Situation

Teaching would be much easier if all schools and all grade levels were identical. Then a standardized curriculum with detailed lesson plans would work everywhere. The fact is, however, that our teaching situations have some similarities—and some definite differences! These differences include class size, facilities, class frequency, equipment, length of the class period, and a broad range of ages, abilities, and special needs within the same class of children. This chapter briefly describes some ways the content in this book can be adapted to various teaching situations to best meet the needs of the children and also to heighten their enjoyment and learning.

Class Size

Although it is recommended that "physical education classes contain the same number of children as the classrooms (e.g., 25 children per class)" (Council on Physical Education for Children, 1992), some schools and districts schedule two or three classes at the same time, which means the PE teacher must teach 60 or more children simultaneously. Although this makes the teacher's job difficult, there are ways teachers can develop the content to provide children with positive (albeit far from ideal) learning experiences. For example, the use of stations, or learning centers, is probably one of the more efficient ways to organize large groups of children (Graham, 1992). And using written directions can minimize the time spent talking to the children, who often seem less inclined to listen when they are in large groups. Also, the teacher must devote substantial time to teaching management routines (Siedentop, 1991) or protocols (Graham, 1992) so that classes run efficiently with minimal interruptions.

Equipment

One reason why large class sizes are *not* recommended is that most physical education programs do not have sufficient equipment—not even for 25 or 30 children. Consequently, if teachers are not careful, the children spend considerable time waiting for turns rather than actually moving. But innovative teachers have discovered ways to maximize practice opportunities for children, even with limited equipment.

Equipment needs to be appropriate to the size and strength of the children. Equipment that is too heavy or too big can hinder game play. There are many distributors who can supply just about anything one needs. Lowering the basket, allowing a wider goal, using smaller and softer soccer balls, changing to smaller basketballs, and using lighter bats are simple ways to accommodate differences. Despite what some say, lowering the basket will not result in problems later when the children shoot at 10-foot baskets.

If sufficient equipment is not available, several alternatives are possible. You can borrow equipment from another school and trade equipment that is available. I have found this to be an excellent way to increase quantity and types of equipment in times of tight budgets. The extra time and effort to make trades benefits the children's learning. Each teacher needs to plan long-range so that the equipment traded is not needed during the trading period. I was involved in such exchanging while teaching in northern Ohio. At first, we transported the equipment in our own cars and an occasional truck. School maintenance workers took over the task of transporting larger equipment. During the 5-year period before I left that district, we were able to completely trade gymnastics equipment and mats to provide a superior gymnastics program for four schools.

Many elementary physical educators are, by necessity, pack rats; they collect almost anything that can possibly be used for instructional purposes. There are many possible sources; I'll mention only a few. One source is the children. Children can be asked to bring in equipment for use in class. During an unlimited refuse pickup, I asked the children to check the piles of unwanted "junk," looking for "gems" for the program. Old but usable balls and other materials were brought in. Some I had to throw away; some needed repair; some could be used in the condition in which they arrived. I remember one old volleyball, with its cover off and the undercover about half worn through. This recovery item became the best volleyball until it wore out 2 years later. It was so much lighter and softer than regulation volleyballs, especially the cheaper rubber ones. There may be treasure in other people's discards. I have had children bring in milk jugs (scoops, markers); old socks (balls) and nylons and coat hangers (paddles); yarn remnants (yarn balls); and nylon string remnants (goals), to name a few pack rat ideas.

Parents and adults in the community are another source of equipment. Contact community members and ask them to check over unused equipment that could be used for games (or other) instruction. I have been fortunate to have several parents make portable goals, an electric timer, and paddles. In some cases, I supplied the materials. In others, I simply gave specifications and the equipment was made from materials that the parents had on hand. One set of 24 paddles was delivered in wrapping paper by the children of a disabled parent who had spent considerable time over several months to make a contribution.

It's amazing what other people have that they might be willing to donate. The middle school and high school physical educators, as well as school teams, may be discarding equipment that has some life left. The industrial arts teacher may be able to design a sound educational project for some students that could result in new and needed equipment for your program. Contacting businesses for discards and possible donations has also been helpful. One plant manager called me and asked if I could use foam rubber protectors that were used to transport glass jars. I was amazed to see a variety of foam shapes that could be used without modification for catching and striking. Another time, numerous partially full cans of spray paint, some water-soluble, were being thrown out. A former student remembered that we had paint needs and asked the boss for permission to take the cans to our school.

There are also many equipment items that must be purchased and that are relatively expensive. The school PTO or other similar group is another avenue of possible help (see Figure 2.1).

Facilities

Although some teachers have adequate indoor and outdoor space, others are less fortunate. In fact, some teachers have no indoor space whatsoever. Others have no grassy areas. Following are some ideas and suggestions for how the content in this book can be adapted for limited indoor or outdoor space.

The problem of sufficient space is a bigger one than is equipment. When children are working on skills or playing games in pairs or in small groups, each of the 4 to 15 groups needs space. Lack of enough space is the most frequently cited limitation teachers talk about when considering small-group play. Changing to plastic bats, balls that don't bounce as much, or sponge balls rather than tennis balls can enable children to work in smaller spaces.

Some games need outdoor space and are extremely restricted if played indoors. It is not uncommon to move soccer play indoors and resort to scooter soccer, crab soccer, or sideline soccer. But it would seem more prudent to work on skills or change activities and return to soccer when the weather permitted.

Figure 2.1 Several ways you can get equipment for your physical education classes.

If adequate space is not available, some adjustments may be necessary. If a game is designed for 2 people, we could add 2 other children, 1 as a coach/helper and 1 to rotate into the game. Instead of 15 games, we would only need 10 for a class of 30. In a 3-on-2 game, we might add 2 or 3 additional children. Instead of needing six areas for 30 children, we could get by with four areas. If the space is so limited that groups cannot achieve well and there is a safety danger, it is better to change activities to fitness, dance, or gymnastics.

Small-group play decreases game complexity, increases numbers of turns, helps maximum participation, aids probability of success, promotes more equitable ability play, and helps children learn strategy. That is easy to understand. What is harder to see is that small-group play can result in more effective use of space. If four badminton nets can be set up so that the width of the playing area is about 5 feet, 2 players can still use the entire length of the court. Three pairs can use one regulation playing area with a buffer of 3 to 4 feet between each playing area (see Figure 2.2). Perhaps we haven't stretched our own imaginations enough to solve the problem of inadequate space. We have, I think, been encapsulated inside what is needed for regulation sports and games.

In some situations, side space or stage space can be used for activity. If playing games in this space is not desirable or feasible, stations (Graham, 1992) may be useful. While you work with the game or games, other children could

participate in fitness, skill, or knowledge activities in these other smaller spaces; children could rotate into game play during the lesson. Task cards, audiotape recorders, or peer teachers can be used for this auxiliary instruction. To save time, warm-up exercises and running laps may need to be discarded (Graham, 1992).

When facilities are extremely limited, teachers must make difficult decisions. Rather than teach games poorly because of inadequate space, a teacher may be justified in restricting play to outdoor space or eliminating games play if space is so inadequate that full-speed play is dangerous or so limiting that no real learning occurs. A facilities problem may only permit large-group activities (fitness, aerobic activities, etc.).

Class Frequency and Length

Schools and classes differ in the number of days per week that the children attend physical education classes and in the length of the classes. Children who have physical education every day for 30 minutes can be expected to learn more than children who only have 60 minutes of physical education each week. This is one reason it is virtually impossible to suggest a standardized physical education curriculum. As suggested later in this chapter in the section on planning, you will need to consider these factors as you plan. Aim to organize and teach your classes so that if students have physical education twice a week for 30 minutes, they receive more than

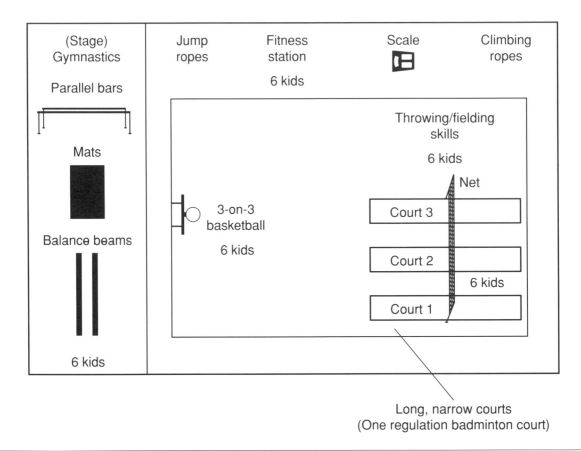

Figure 2.2 Use available space creatively.

16 hours of actual learning time each year (Kelly, 1989).

Time is the most limiting factor on program quality, content variety and depth, and integration of skills. In a program that meets only once a week, teachers must make even more careful content decisions than I stressed in chapter 1. In such limited programs, teachers may need to take most of the curricular time for manipulation skills or games or restrict the content to skill development with little, if any, development of games playing as advocated in chapters 3 and 4. This is unfortunate, but at least the children learn single and combination skills, with some application of these skills in simple situations. This is preferable to playing games and not developing games skills and strategies. In other words, playing games based on rules rather than on learning strategies is not a good use of curricular time—especially if there is insufficient time to teach prerequisite manipulation skills to the proficiency needed for success in games.

If programs have very limited time for learning to play games, restricting games play to small-group, beginning offensive and defensive strategy learning may be necessary. In these situations, teachers may need to forget about building up to regulation play or even other games that require complicated strategies and rules. Programs that meet three or more times a week require a broader variety of games. There may be enough time to include strategies, building to more complicated games play.

Accommodating Individual Differences

Many classes today have children with special needs who are mainstreamed (i.e., their physical education class is scheduled with another class). In some instances you can accommodate children with special needs (not only those who are mainstreamed) by techniques such as *teaching by invitation* or *intratask variation* (Graham, 1992). In other instances it may be necessary to make different adaptations to accommodate the needs of these students. Some accommodations that teachers can make for children when teaching games are discussed in this section.

Varying the equipment may help meet the needs of individual children. This can be as simple as allowing choices of various kinds of equipment or as complex as designing special equipment for a particular individual. In skill teaching, providing tasks that have several entry levels or using problem solving have such accommodation built in (see Figure 2.3).

In actual games playing, meeting individual special needs without significantly changing the game can be a challenge. Two general ways are easy to administer. One way happens naturally because of the small-group play. Children tend to choose others of similar ability in partner and small-group game play. With the option to work at combination skills *or* play a competitive game, children may elect to work more cooperatively in skill practice. Riley (1975) found that such an approach resulted in children being more sensitive to children of varying skill abilities. A second way involves a version of uneven-sided games (Graham, 1992), in which a child can be a member of opposing offenses. This way, for example, a visually impaired child can play for both teams, giving the child more time and opportunity to make decisions and hone his or her motor skills.

If a games approach involves having children analyze games and part of the time design their own games, the children should be reminded to consider individual differences and children with special needs. Morris (1976, 1980) and Morris and Stiehl (1989) help children design games that emphasize including *all* children in the game. Riley (1975) found that a humanistic games approach resulted in children focusing on trying to make the game work rather than just winning. Both of these approaches to games, and the emphasis in this book on fairness and respecting others, can help meet individual differences. This is not an easy task, but it is important.

Planning

Chapter 3 contains an overview of the content that can be developed through the learning experiences in chapters 6 to 10. An important decision you must make as a teacher is how much of the content described in this book to use in your program. Remember, this is only one of five books (Buschner, 1994; Purcell, 1994; Ratliffe & Ratliffe, 1994; Werner, 1994) that describe the content of physical education for children. Ideally, your program will include content from each of the areas, so you have some difficult decisions to make. A complete outline for planning is provided in *Teaching Children Physical Education* (Graham, 1992), but only you can develop the plans that will work best at your school. Also included in this book are benchmarks (Franck et al., 1991) that relate specifically to this content area. Use these benchmarks to help decide which aspects of the content are most important for your children to learn (see Figure 1.4).

Another important planning factor is the length of time you have taught the children. Your

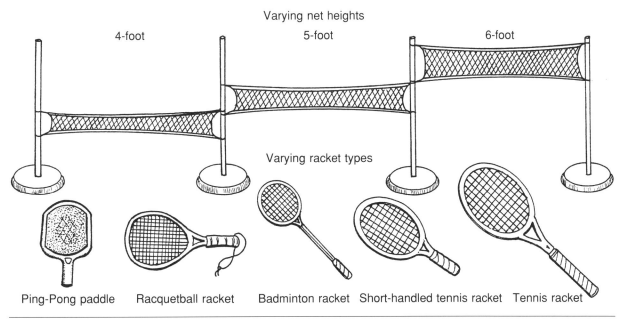

Figure 2.3 Accommodate individual differences by offering a variety of equipment.

plans will (and should) be different for the first year of a program than for the tenth year. When you have worked with fifth or sixth graders from the time they started school, they will be able to do, and will know, different things than the fifth and sixth graders did your first year at that school.

Summary

One of the most valid criticisms of physical education programs has been that they were designed only for athletes—and were a painful experience for those who were poorly skilled. Contemporary physical educators are moving away from this one-model-fits-all pattern of restrictive physical education toward programs that are adjusted, adapted, and designed specifically to match the abilities, interests, and needs of individual children. This chapter describes some of the considerations that contemporary teachers take into account when designing programs specifically for the children at their schools.

Chapter 3

Incorporating Games Into Your Program

Children need to possess basic skills to achieve the program's goals in games instruction. These skills comprise a large portion of the content in the primary years. (For more information on skills instruction, see *Teaching Children Movement Concepts and Skills* by Craig Buschner, 1994.) Manipulation skills crucial to becoming a good games player involve sending objects away, receiving objects, and controlling objects while moving. Thus, combinations of catching and throwing, controlling an object, dribbling, striking, and other skills are prerequisite to game play. In actual game play, these skills need to be automatic or nearly automatic. If not, the game proceeds at a slow and awkward pace. The children direct so much attention to performing the skills that they have little or no attention left to focus on strategies and cooperating with teammates.

Categories of Games

What games should I teach? This is the question all teachers ask. But it is the wrong question to ask *first*. Initially teachers should ask about the nature of games and how games relate to children's development. Then teachers should ask about what's in a game, how games are structured, and the sequence for teaching games.

Then the question becomes, How can I teach games that are consistent with the rationale based on answers to these other questions? And if a player is trying to become a good games player, what kinds of games should he or she learn?

These are difficult questions, especially the last one. The games should focus on decision making, strategy, and applying manipulation skills. Five categories of games are presented in this book. One kind is tag games. The other four were proposed by Thorpe, Bunker, and Almond (1986) and expanded by Werner and Almond (1990). These categories include target; net and wall; invasion; and fielding games. Without a way to group games into categories, a teacher can easily select and teach games in haphazard order. These categories allow teachers to plan for progression within a category of games and to include work on strategies that can transfer to similar activities.

Tag Games

Instruction in this category begins with chasing, fleeing, and dodging activities (Buschner, 1994); control of an object is added in subsequent games. Tag games are a simple and useful form of strategy games. The purpose is to move, change direction, and dodge to (a) tag someone or cause others to lose control of an object or (b) avoid being tagged or keep others from interfering with the object being controlled. In this book this category is much more limited than the popular conception of tag games. Tag games included here have movement and strategy objectives. Many popular tag games (e.g., freeze tag and stoop tag) are excluded. Also excluded are games with 1 It and 30 other children running, games with high waiting times, and any kind of elimination tag game (Graham, 1992, p. 142).

Target Games

Activities and games that focus on targets emphasize accuracy in sending an object to a particular area. Games involving skill in aiming can be active, moving games, but popular examples have limited or no locomotion by the sender (bowling, golf, archery). Simpler forms involve striking, kicking, and throwing objects toward targets. Many target games involve relatively limited body moving, running, and dodging. In target games, such as free throw shooting, golf, archery, and horseshoes, participants decide when to begin the activity and control the pace. Many of the other four categories of games require participants to adjust skill and strategy after the activity begins. Target games tend to have closed environments, whereas the other game categories have more open, changing environments.

Net and Wall Games

Net and wall games involve moving and controlling an object and making it difficult for other people to gain possession or send the object back to the wall or across a net. Tennis and volleyball are sport examples; foursquare is a simple example. Net and wall games, even adult forms, often require fewer players than do invasion games. Only 2 to 4 players are needed for many of these games, and often less space is needed than for invasion games.

Players in net and wall games control a fixed area. They move about in the space to position themselves to best cover the opponent's return throw or hit. Often this means returning to a recommended position rather than moving to a new position. Defenders in net and wall games adjust their positions in relation to the location of the offense and the ball.

Invasion Games

Invasion games focus on controlling an object in a specified area. They include simple keep-away games in which 2 or more players attempt to keep control of an object while 1 or more other players try to intercept the moving object or tag the player who has possession of the object. In more complicated invasion games, one group tries to control the ball or object and move through the space to a goal line or goal area, invading the other group's space. When this occurs, one side has an advantage; this side has the ball and is typically on offense, but not always. Usually offense involves scoring, so I label this as "*ahh! fence*" because shooting and scoring is awe-inspiring. The other group is guarding some space or goal and is on defense. The defenders present an obstacle to the offense, so I call this "*da fence*" (and picture a white picket fence). Figure 3.1 illustrates these concepts.

Fielding Games

In fielding games typically an object is sent into an area, and the sender tries to run somewhere, and possibly return, before the fielders can get the object and send it to a specified place. Rules are specific to the game in adult versions, such as cricket and baseball, and are complicated.

In simple play, games may be limited to fielding and running and can resemble tag games. There is considerable positioning in the field in relation to where teammates and the runner or runners are located. Learning to back up throws is also an important phase of fielding games. The official versions of these games involve 9 or more players on each team. This number presents problems in elementary physical education programs because students spend too much time waiting and have few practice attempts. In an analysis of a fourth-grade kickball game, Wilson (1976) found extremely high management and waiting times; very few turns for most children; no turns fielding for many children, especially girls; and high dominance by the teacher. The kickball problems (Wilson, 1976) also are present with large-group games in softball, baseball, and cricket. Although smaller-group games are recommended, problems of objects' interfering with other groups' space need to be minimized.

Figure 3.1   "Ahh! fence" and "da fence."

Learning Games Strategy

Learning strategy in games is different than learning movement skills. Often during games, teachers focus on how the children perform the skills, but the focus should be on strategy. If a teacher realizes that low game quality is mainly because of skill performance, several options exist. The teacher can (a) continue the activity for a while so that the children get the general idea of the game, (b) move back to Stage 2 and have the children practice combining the skills without the pressure of strategy, or (c) change the skills to simple (automatic) ones so that the children can concentrate on strategy.

Strategy is deciding when to do something to achieve an objective. Sometimes the term *tactics* is used to describe this cognitive decision making. Knowledge of tactics, or cognitive ideas of what to do and when to do it, is strategy. Which strategies are basic and come first? Which are easiest to learn? Which strategies are intermediate ones? Advanced ones? In the next section, strategies are listed for each of the five types of games. The examples are limited to basic tactics.

Strategies for Tag Games

Very basic strategies will be explained because the examples in this category of games are simplex (very simple). The strategies are based on the following skills, which children are already familiar with outside of game play:

1. Stay balanced at all times, ready to move in any direction.
2. Use a variety of fakes when tagging and when avoiding tags.
3. Change directions and speeds quickly in dodging.
4. Be aware of what is happening to the sides and to the back, too.

Children have previously practiced many of these strategies in learning pieces without the tagging aspect. In catching, children practiced balancing and holding positions, as well as maintaining ready positions for receiving objects. Staying balanced, with weight on the front part of the feet, which are about shoulder-width apart, is necessary in tag games to move to tag others and to move to avoid others (see Figure 3.2). Copying others' movements and doing the opposite of what they do is good practice for faking. Children need to be skilled at pretending to move one way and then moving the other way, with various parts of the body and with the entire body.

Actually faking is intertwined with changing directions and speeds quickly and dodging. An important strategy here is to watch the person's hips and middle, rather than the limb and head movements. The head often is used for faking, as are many body parts. In tag games, and later in many other kinds of games, being alert and knowing what is going on to the sides and behind oneself is important. Simple tag games may be ideal for learning this alertness.

Figure 3.2   Ready position for tag games.

Strategies for Target Games

In target games the performer plans what to do and when to begin. Because play is self-paced, this decision making differs from that of games in which something in the environment changes rapidly, causing an immediate reaction decision. Basic target strategies include the following:

1. Take time to stay as relaxed and confident as is possible.
2. Don't be hurried; determine when you want to begin.
3. Assess your own skill and the situation to decide whether to try for extreme accuracy or play safer.
4. Concentrate as clearly as you can; be focused.

The main strategy issue for target games is whether to go for extreme accuracy or play it safe. In elementary physical education, one strategy is to decide whether to score more times in easier target areas or fewer times in harder targets (see Figure 3.3). Students need to be able to compare point values and target difficulty to make strategy decisions. Another strategy is involved when defending a free shot; both the player trying to score and the defender need to watch each other carefully to anticipate each other's movements.

Strategies for Net and Wall Games

In a way, net and wall games are simple: The playing space is constant, the net or wall provides a focal point, and positioning has central importance. There are general rules for positioning and repositioning, and the playing area is easy to visualize. The following five strategies are basic to net and wall games:

1. Send objects to the wall or across the net to the most open areas.
2. Begin in and after every return reposition to the area that provides the best coverage.
3. Vary play so that opponents cannot easily anticipate what will happen.
4. Share coverage of the area with teammates.
5. Communicate with teammates so that teammates can help each other.

Although these five strategies are important for beginners, complex and intricate versions of these same five strategies are vital to high-level competitive play. During the upper elementary years, teaching should focus on the basic strategies as the children are ready for them.

Learning *to send the ball to open areas or spaces that cannot be easily defended* is a key to becoming a good player. Changing the area and shape of the playing space will help children learn this concept. In a wide area, angling one's returns is important; in deep, narrow playing space, sending opponents back and then near is the best strategy (see Figure 3.4). Players should adjust this basic strategy depending on where the opponent is and where the opponent is going or is likely to go. A team is in control when the opponents must run in many different directions just to reach and play a ball.

In many net and wall games, players need to *position themselves for the best coverage* and follow a general rule of moving back to the center of the playing area. However, deciding where to play also depends on how the opponent is likely to send the return, and from where. To adjust his or her position in relation to the probable return, the player must analyze what's happening and then adjust position. If the player gets out of position, the only strategy left is to guess from where the ball is coming and hope the guess is correct.

In net and wall games, *varying what one is doing* is essential. This means changing how one sends the ball so that opponents cannot easily predict what will happen. Players should plan and execute (with appropriate faking, too) different kinds of hits, kicks, or throws. Then opponents can't set up early in advantageous positions and make easy returns; they can't predict

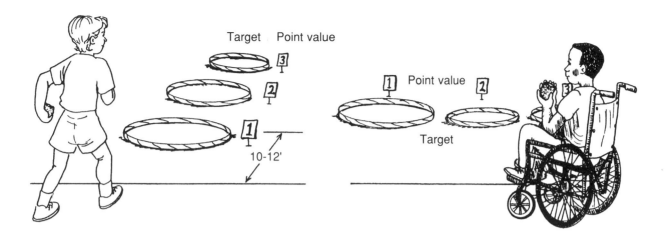

Figure 3.3   One strategy in target games involves determining whether to try for easy or difficult target areas.

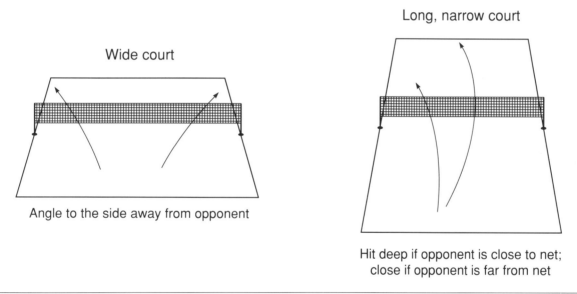

Figure 3.4   Strategy for net and wall games includes determining which areas or spaces cannot be easily defended by opponents.

well but must wait or guess. In combination skill learning, emphasis should be on variety in receiving and sending objects, including changes in directions, heights, speeds, and force. The more combinations and variety a player can do, the more options he or she has in net and wall games.

The first three basic strategy ideas—send objects to open areas, position yourself, and vary play—can be used in partner games, and also in group play. In addition, two other basic strategies are needed for group play. One is *sharing coverage and use of space* with 1 or more partners, which is really an extension of the second

strategy. There are more restrictions on and responsibilities for space use when players have 1 or more partners. Teammates must decide where to play to provide best coverage. They need to play their own areas and not go into a teammate's area if the teammate is in position and ready to play the object. When a partner is playing the ball, the teammate should position either to back up that player in case of a miss *or* to provide the best support coverage. Especially in games like volleyball, players must reposition for coverage depending on which team has the ball and from where on the court the other team must send it across the net. Teaching children to continually position and reposition *during* game play is a difficult and long process.

The second teammate strategy is linked with positioning, namely, *talking with teammates so that they know what each is trying to do.* With serving and some other strategies, this exchange can occur in private conferences before or after a play or point begins. The simplest communication is about who will play the ball, but this often must be decided during actual play. Who will play balls that are in the boundary space between 2 players is such a problem. Many other messages need to be sent before and during game play—such as that a teammate is backing up, where that person is positioned, or whether to play a ball or let it go out-of-bounds. Such communication is not easy to achieve. Rather than tell children where to play, structure a learning piece so that the children make these decisions—or at least have them evaluate whether where they were and what they did were beneficial or needed improvement.

Strategies for Invasion Games

The ability to dodge and change direction quickly while maintaining one's balance is essential in invasion games. Children can learn these skills by participating in dance, gymnastics, and tag games. And many of the strategies basic to net and wall games can be used in invasion games. In invasion games, the actual playing area changes by the moment and in unpredictable ways. Perhaps less accuracy in sending objects is needed than in net games because teammates are moving and can cover lower passing accuracy by slowing down or speeding up. In any case, having moving sets of players on offense and on defense requires a different overall strategy than that used in net and wall games. The many types of invasion games, the different kinds of equipment, and the emphasis on combinations of kicking, dribbling, throwing, catching, and striking result in many rules and skill variations.

The following five strategies are basic to invasion games:

1. Create open space and reposition to gain an advantage.
2. Guard space and reposition to deny or close space.
3. Guard opponents to interfere with their movements or object manipulation.

4. Move an object into more advantageous space to reach a specified area or to score points.
5. Communicate with and use teammates effectively.

It's easy to assume that children know and can do the strategies or that mentioning them once is enough to teach them. But when the emphasis in teaching games changes from rules and regulations to strategy, teachers realize just how complex playing games is.

In the first strategy, *creating space* requires that *one position oneself and then frequently reposition* to gain and keep an advantage. Primary school children can begin learning this by moving to open spaces, sharing space, and keeping away from others. In invasion games, faking to draw an opponent one way and then going another is effective. Children and inexperienced players position themselves almost anywhere and then stay there, hoping for a chance to catch that coveted ball or object. Moving to get open is essential. Moving when one does not have the ball is a difficult concept to understand and even more difficult to do during games (see Figure 3.5). Of particular importance to offense is changing direction abruptly and at very sharp angles, especially if the defense is going at a constant speed in one direction.

For the second strategy, the defensive team attempts to reduce open spaces, to deny or *close space* by positioning and repositioning. One way is for the player to be an obstacle, or a fence, causing an offensive player to slow down, change direction, and take more time to reach his or

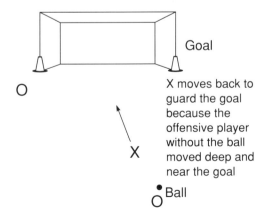

Figure 3.5 Invasion games strategy involves positioning and repositioning to gain advantage over the opponent.

her destination. In games, achieving this may be enough to cause an errant pass. Or it may upset the flow and timing of the offense just enough, for example, to keep them from having enough advantage to score, forcing them to move the ball to a less open teammate, or interfering with a good passing lane. Defenders must move and position themselves within the game rules by getting to an area and setting a position before the offensive person gets there. This is positioning in front of the opponent; the defender also, as a general strategy, tries to stay between the opponent and the goal. Defenders, like offensive players, need to position themselves in relation not only to the particular person being guarded, but to the positions of the other offensive players and the location of the ball.

Related to defensive positioning is the third strategy, *guarding an opponent*. Defenders must not only guard space; they also need to develop strategies to guard against another player or players. In addition to positioning oneself between the offensive player and the goal, defenders must make important space decisions depending on how far from the goal or ball an offensive player is. Three possible defensive options are (a) staying close enough to cause the offense some difficulty (à la "da fence"), (b) trying to intercept the ball when there is a good chance to accomplish this, or (c) moving close to and in front of the opponent to keep that person from even receiving a pass. Varying what one is doing, using fakes, changing speeds, and changing one's defensive body shape make a defender unpredictable and difficult to play against. A defensive player also needs to be able to reduce space between oneself and an offensive person quickly but then slow down as he or she gets close so that the person with the ball cannot dodge easily. This is a basic defensive strategy that children can use to become better players.

The goalkeeper has special skills and strategies to learn. He or she defends space by making his or her body into wide, tall, and solid shapes; the ability to make these reactions rapidly is important. Goalkeepers must be able to set up in the direction of the most likely shot and decide when to move out toward an attacker. When defenders assist the goalie, the goalie needs to tell these defenders where to move or whom to guard. When there is no teammate to help, the goalie may need to move out toward the attacker who has the ball, which can force a weak or hurried shot and cut down the possible shooting angles. This is very hard for beginners to understand

and do. In any case, goalkeepers have special skills and strategies to learn.

The fourth strategy, *controlling and moving an object when someone else is trying to take the object from you*, presents exciting challenges, especially if both players have comparable ability. Varying the way one passes, receives, dribbles, fakes, positions, and visually focuses adds to one's offensive skills and increases one's ability if passes are accurate and sent to open teammates. The player with the ball should follow the recommended priority sequence: First, try to score if there is a high probability that a score will occur; second, pass to a teammate in better scoring position or to an open teammate if one is guarded closely; third, move and continue to control the ball by oneself, such as by dribbling, while looking for open teammates. If children focus entirely on the third priority aspect without looking to pass, the game is too difficult or the child needs further instruction about why this priority sequence is necessary.

The direction in which the ball is moved is also important. Luxbacher (1991) recommends moving the ball directly to the goal and in a straight line, if possible. It's better to move the ball inside rather than outside and away from the goal, because that way the ball is getting closer to the goal. These strategies are the two most direct ways of getting an object close for a good chance to score, but the defense will try to prevent them.

Communicating with and using teammates effectively is important in controlling and moving the ball. Teammates must let each other know what they are doing and what they want teammates to do. Verbal messages are important, as are visual ones, including body gestures. Having signals to indicate what to do gives the attackers an advantage. Defenders can also use verbal and nonverbal messages and signals. If teachers consider communication to be a beginning and crucial step in learning teamwork, games instruction will vary considerably from the traditional emphasis on rules and regulations. If children are unwilling to share verbally, I doubt they will share the ball, learn strategy, or develop teamwork.

Communication with teammates may be even more important for the defense. Telling teammates where one is, that one is coming, whom one is guarding, or where one should go are examples of necessary communication on defense. Defenders can also help teammates by keeping the ball away from the middle and in front of the goal, forcing the ball to the outside and near a sideline so little space is available. If a teammate is moving to guard the ball, one can support the teammate by moving back a little, trying to get in the way to intercept a pass (see Figure 3.6). Positioning to slow down the offense while waiting for teammates to get there and help is another way defenders can assist teammates.

Children also need to apply what they've learned, and they're more likely to do so if they understand the rationale behind the concept. If children understand that spreading out and using the available space has advantages, they will do it. When a player passes to a teammate who moved and signaled for the ball, that reinforces the chances that the teammate will do the same when the passer signals. The support that comes from spreading out needs to be discussed and reinforced, for offense and for defense. The children need to understand that positioning players at angles and triangles helps space coverage, allows passing lanes (i.e., passways) and coverage of these lanes, and aids communication (see Figure 3.6).

The basic strategies for invasion games are quite comprehensive. Teachers need to analyze the strategies that need to be taught and choose or devise a game that focuses on those strategies. Or teachers (or students) need to emphasize one or two strategies for a particular game and then extend these strategies as skills develop.

Strategies for Fielding Games

Many of the strategies for tag games and invasion games can be used in games built around fielding and throwing, running, striking, and kicking. So only a few strategies specific to fielding games will be emphasized here. Basic strategies for fielding games include the following:

1. Send objects into open spaces.
2. Position for best coverage of the playing area.
3. Reposition to back up teammates.

Batters and kickers need to send balls into *open spaces*, just as in invasion and net and wall games. The general idea is to send balls low, hard, and straight so that fielders have difficulty catching them. Players may also hit balls to force fielders to run, such as in bunting or hitting for distance.

Positioning for best coverage requires fielders, as in invasion games, to decide where to begin in order to best cover the field, depending on what batters tend to do. All the fielding examples ask children to think and plan how to position most effectively.

Repositioning in invasion games is done to open or close spaces. In fielding games, *repositioning is done primarily to back up teammates* or to cover an area from which a teammate moved away. Various situations require this backing up. The progression of difficulty can be seen by comparing the game 300 and regulation baseball. In many adult fielding games, almost every throw involves backing up the receiver.

Summary

Game play involves learning strategies and communicating and cooperating with teammates.

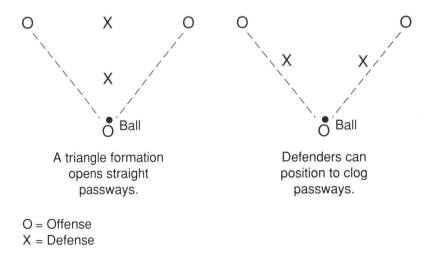

A triangle formation
opens straight
passways.

Defenders can
position to clog
passways.

O = Offense
X = Defense

Figure 3.6 Effective communication with teammates enables players to clog opponents' passways.

Children need to first develop prerequisite skills so that they can focus on strategies and the complexities of game play. In this book games are classified into tag, target, net and wall, invasion, and fielding types. Each has specific strategies that are learned in much the same way that game skills are learned. To accomplish this, there must be progression in learning strategy, too.

Basic strategies are explained for each of the categories of games. The categories have similarities and differences in strategy. Strategies within a category integrate and reinforce each other; they are not isolated concepts. The strategies in this chapter form the basis for instruction in beginning offensive and defensive game play in elementary school physical education.

Chapter 4

Principles for Teaching Games

Content in games instruction is based on games stages, which were described in chapter 1. Games structure and strategies are necessary for optimal learning. This chapter begins with criteria for selecting and evaluating games. Next I discuss the structure of games and concepts that are important for children to learn and use. How children can modify games, and even design their own games, is the third main topic. Finally, the impact of games organization on learning is discussed.

How to Select and Evaluate Games

Many games are available to elementary teachers. It is easy to choose a game that another teacher recommends or one that reads as though it would be fun. Choosing games that are developmentally appropriate and educationally sound may not be so easy. We need some definite criteria for evaluating and selecting games. In traditional PE the most important criterion was whether the teacher thought that a game had value. But opinions of individual teachers are subjective. You may think that a game is important, and another teacher may think that the same game has no value whatsoever. To make progress, we must move beyond evaluating games based mainly on personal interest, past experience, or similar assessments. The criteria shown in Table 4.1 are a framework for evaluating already-designed games.

We can use these questions to evaluate whether a particular game is valuable enough to be included in the curriculum. If the answer to all or most of the questions is yes, then that game might easily be played. If the answer to all or most of these questions is no, the teacher has three options: Exclude the game, modify the game to meet the criteria so that the modified game is educationally sound, or consider an alternative that can achieve the same objective.

Table 4.1 Criteria to Evaluate Games

Does the game

Provide for maximum participation, giving all children many, high-quality turns?

Provide for safe play?

Focus on skills and strategy considered to be "good to learn"?

Meet the needs of children with varying abilities?

Support a developmental principle?

Encourage efficient and effective movement?

Build on skills, concepts, and strategies learned previously?

Use skills, concepts, and strategies to help children become better games players?

Enhance social and emotional status, including humane considerations of individuals and their differing abilities?

In addition to the teacher's using these criteria, children can learn to apply these criteria to evaluate games, too. To do so, the children must understand the criteria and how to use them accurately. This will take considerable time but will empower the children. They can begin to control the games, rather than the games controlling them. These criteria are aspects of games that children need to know. At first children can apply these evaluative ideas to assess games that are already structured and taught in the elementary physical education program. Next they can evaluate games in the classroom and on the playground; later children could analyze games and sports in the community and in the culture. Morris (1980) and Morris and Stiehl (1989), among others, advocate this process as essential in elementary programs. Let's discuss in more detail each of the criteria used to evaluate games.

Does the Game Encourage Maximum Participation?

Is the game organized so that the children can have a high number of chances; that is, does the game encourage maximum participation (Figley, Mitchell, & Wright, 1986)? Is there adequate equipment to ensure maximum participation? Does the organization promote most children being active much of the time and involved in the skills and strategies? Many popular games have 1 child who is It or one ball for 30 children. Such games should be used sparingly, if at all. This is a rather easy point to evaluate, but it's more difficult to determine whether a game provides many turns for all children. Some games have all the children participating, but the waiting time is so high that the children cannot possibly receive enough chances to really learn the skill or strategy. This should be evident to teachers, but it is easy to select games in which most children get few turns and wait in line a long time between turns. Kickball is such a game. Wilson (1976) analyzed kickball during a fourth-grade lesson and found that each child kicked the ball twice, and about 35% of the children never fielded a ball. Surely, we can do better than this.

Is the Game Safe?

Are the game and its rules safe? Does the equipment or its use have any unsafe or dangerous aspects? Could the movements required in the game cause a child to be injured? Safety is an important concern in evaluating games. Games such as Red Rover, in which children try to break through a line of children standing side by side with hands joined, can result in arm and shoulder injuries. This game has no educational value, is dangerous, and should never be played in physical education. All games have a possibility for injury, but there is no need, especially in this litigious society, to choose games that are inherently dangerous. Also, children need to be taught to respect the safety and rights of others during all games.

Does the Game Teach Anything Useful?

Does the game emphasize effective skills and strategies? Many simple tag games are fun but teach little about moving well, changing direction quickly, and dodging. Squirrels in Trees is a game in which a third of the children run to find a "tree" formed by 2 other children holding hands. There are one or two too few trees so 1 or 2 children are left without a tree each round. The game is fun, but aside from learning to follow directions and to play different roles, what does it teach about moving, learning to control one's body, and being a good games player? Many line games and circle games could be designed to focus on what it means to dodge someone else or what part of the body to watch when trying to prevent another person from dodging. But this isn't done in these games, or even explained in many texts.

Does the Game Meet the Needs of Children With Varying Abilities?

Is the game designed or can the game be modified to meet the needs of individual children with differing abilities? Are equipment choices available so that individual skill, size, and developmental differences are taken into account? Do rules allow for the inclusion of all children? Can the game be modified for children of high skill and low skill? In a games program designed to answer these questions with a yes, games in the same class or lesson might use different equipment and groups of varying sizes. Although all games focus on a particular strategy, games designed to be appropriate for children with varying abilities have varying complexities of strategy or rules.

Does the Game Adhere to Developmental Principles?

Is the game congruent with and based on what is known about children's growth and development (Williams, 1983; Belka, 1990)? Call Ball (which I discussed earlier) probably violates several developmental principles. Children playing circle tag games often veer way outside the running track; that is, they run off at a tangent. This may indicate that the children have not had sufficient experience in running straight, then in slightly curved patterns, then in tighter circles. In batting and fielding games, do children have adequate experience catching lower-arced balls before they are asked to catch high-arced balls in the outfield?

Does the Game Encourage Efficient and Effective Movement?

Does the game involve movement that is mechanically sound and leads to better movement? Figley et al. (1986) discuss the game Nervous Wreck, in which 1 player has a ball in the middle of a circle of others. The players must catch any ball thrown toward them. But if they move, blink, or prepare to catch when the ball is *not* thrown or when it is faked toward them, they are eliminated from the game. But good players prepare and get ready to catch by changing their stance, facing the direction of the throw, and adjusting the positions of their hands and arms. Nervous Wreck works against the way we would like players to prepare to catch an object; the game even penalizes the reflex action of blinking—this is not consistent with basic physiology. Games such as Nervous Wreck have no value in a developmentally appropriate curriculum. Another game, Circle Stride Ball, has children stand side by side with legs straddled. The object is to push (another version is kick) a ball past the other children. This wide position is difficult to maintain, and the stationary position requirement is not related to actual goalie play. Such games should be eliminated or modified to allow more natural and effective practice.

Does the Game Build on Previous Instruction?

Are skills, concepts, and strategies that were emphasized in previous instruction used as a basis for the game? What prerequisites, if any, lead to this game? Does the game have the potential

to challenge skills and strategies for the players, to ask for a higher level of thinking, cooperation, and skill performance? Are these challenges within the abilities of the children at this time? (See Figure 4.1.)

Does the Game Develop Good Players?

This criterion is similar to the last. Does the game teach skills, concepts, or strategies that will enable students to become more proficient games players? Many games can include such emphases that can transfer to other, similar games. Skills, concepts, and strategies can also be prerequisite to more advanced, skillful game play.

Does the Game Enhance Social and Emotional Development?

Is the game likely to enhance the social and emotional status of the children? Does the game even have the potential to do so? As I discussed in chapter 1, the emphasis should be on "allism" rather than elitism, on gender equity, and on social consideration of all involved. Elimination games, unnecessary penalties, and teasing of lower skilled and unorthodox performers should not be part of any game. Asking the winners whether they want to run a victory lap is preferable to having losers run a lap. Perhaps having the winners lead a victory lap but inviting the losing team to join them is even more preferable.

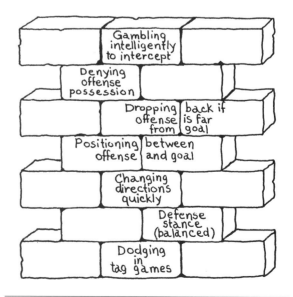

Figure 4.1 Appropriate developmental games build on previous instruction.

The way in which the teacher conducts the class and guides children in expressing winning and losing, celebrating accomplishments, and accepting others' efforts sets the tone for the way children treat each other. Figure 4.2 provides an example of desirable social behavior.

How Games Are Structured

Stage 3 games instruction involves learning basic offensive and defensive strategy. This requires changes from traditional game play, with its regulation playing areas and equipment, official number of players on each team, complex rules, and specialized player roles. Children need to understand and use factors that affect the nature of games. Too often, specific games are taught, but the structure of games is not taught. Morris (1980) explains a number of structural factors that one needs to consider when teaching games. These factors include the following:

- Size of playing area
- Kinds and number of equipment used
- Types of skills used
- Rules
- Number of players
- Organization of players
- Purpose of the game

Children need to know these factors so that they can comprehend how games are designed and structured. When teachers focus primarily on rules and regulations, scoring, and winning, children do not learn the nature of what really constitutes a game. Knowing how games are organized and structured can help children understand games and focus on the educational outcomes we desire.

For example, often I have observed children playing a game with considerably less success than they would have had using a different size playing area. The children did not realize this and, in many cases, were not permitted to change the playing area because a well-meaning adult insisted on using regulation dimensions so that the children would learn to play like adults. Figure 4.3 shows how children can analyze playing area and make changes to improve game quality.

Other factors, in addition to playing area, affect games and have tremendous potential to help elementary children understand the educational values of games (Morris & Stiehl, 1989). Table 4.2 lists examples of these factors from simplex to complex. With the continuing emphasis on organized youth sports, it is crucial to educate children and prospective teachers and coaches about these game-influencing factors. It is no longer sufficient to teach children how to play a large number of games. In an exemplary movement program, elementary children must learn how to become good games players.

In my own formal education, I learned to play a number of games, some fairly well. I did not learn to become an adept, cognitive player. I did

Figure 4.2   Games should enhance social and emotional development by encouraging children to accept others.

Figure 4.3 Children are capable of analyzing games and suggesting modifications for skill level when appropriate.

not learn how to create games that are challenging and fair to all participants. I did not learn how to control games, change games, or create games. I learned how to play games within a structure given to me by teachers and coaches. Thank goodness children seem to invent play activities on their own, at least when they are very young. Wouldn't it be preferable to provide them with skills and knowledge so that they have control of games, rather than being controlled by games? This chapter emphasizes beginning offensive and defensive strategy in Stage 3, which can be taught to children in Grades 3 to 6.

Children Can Analyze and Design Their Own Games

Children who know how can modify and create their own games for a variety of purposes. They can modify games to simplify them or to make them more difficult. In doing so, children begin to use problem solving to think about what they and others are doing in games and, especially, about educational aspects of games (Graham, 1992).

Children can compare games played for educational purposes with games outside of the school, and with professional games and sports. Intermediate school children can benefit from comparing and contrasting different kinds of games, their purposes, and the effects of various play behaviors on others. Doing this leads to skill analysis and helps children realize the tie-in between highly skilled performance and the level of physical fitness needed for that performance. Also, children can analyze whether specific behaviors are considerate of others, fair, or ethical (see Figure 4.4).

Table 4.2 Examples of Factors and Complexity That Affect Game Play

Level of complexity	Players	Equipment	Area used	Rules	Movement	Strategies
Simple	1	Lightweight, soft/foam, short rackets	Specific to skill	Few, simple	None	None
	2		More to cover	More as needed	Move in personal space	One, simple
	3	Junior size, foam balls, light rackets	More crowded for offense			Few, simple
	4	Rubber baseballs	Teammates must communicate	More and intricate	One stationary, one moving	More, increased complexity
	5	Tennis rackets, baseballs, wooden bats	Nearer to regulation	Complex or regulation	Both moving Both moving fast	Many
Complex	>6				All moving All moving fast	Many and more complex

Figure 4.4 Children can analyze whether behavior is appropriate.

To use this process, a teacher whose primary approach has been teacher-centered must alter his or her behavior. Teachers need skill in both direct and indirect teaching styles (Graham, 1992, p. 135). The teacher needs to ask questions, use convergent problem solving, and, to some extent, use divergent problem solving; this approach enables children to think and analyze game content and game behaviors (Graham, 1992, pp. 128-135).

Once they learn factors of game structure, children can analyze games and even transfer their analysis to other games (see Figure 4.5). The objectives of learning about the factors that affect game structure include understanding what is involved in a particular game and learning strategies that are useful to becoming a better games player.

Children can use their creativeness, discovery learning, and knowledge of what factors affect games to invent and design games. At first, these insights might easily be directed toward a particular skill or toward making decisions about equipment and organization. Later, they can consider fairness, inclusion, and equity as well. The games invented can be designed to (a) lead to a specific skill or even to a specific sport, (b) combine skills from specific sports, or (c) be a game that is not specific to any recognizable sport we know.

Guidelines for Children's Decision Making

Initially the process of inventing games takes a lot of time and may not be productive. If I were working with a new group of children, I would first ask them to analyze one aspect of a game we were playing rather than to evaluate the whole game. I would limit their focus and structure the complexity of what I was asking them to do, especially if they had no experience in working in this way. Later when I asked them to design a game, the request would still not be open-ended. I would ask them to design a partner game in a small space with specified equipment, such as a choice of one or two balls, and either a barrel or two hoops so that the ball could be moved back and forth between them.

Later, if the group were larger, I would ask the children to design a game in which all players were moving most or all of the time. In addition, all players would have to play all roles (if different roles were included), and all players would need to control the ball or balls about an equal share of the time. It wouldn't matter if the game were a cooperative one or a competitive one, and I probably wouldn't even mention this to them.

Reviewing the criticisms of traditional games in chapter 1 might help children design games that avoid these criticisms. For example, if a relatively large group of children was designing a game, I might put this requirement on the game development: Make sure that no one waits for a turn. The children must think through any game organization to make sure there is very limited standing and waiting. If more teachers were required to think through games like this, games instruction could be vastly improved almost overnight. If we ask elementary children to think through aspects of games, we better do a lot of similar thinking—or they'll be ahead of us in a flash.

Kathy Pottak, elementary teacher in Pittsburgh, PA, has fifth and sixth graders design original games and then later teach them to the rest of the class. Groups of 4 or 5 children work together during one class period and then have 2 weeks to complete the game and hand in a written description. The children must follow these guidelines:

1. Game safety is a priority.
2. At least two thirds of the class should play at one time.
3. Rules and directions must be easy to explain and understand.
4. Almost any equipment can be used.
5. Games must accommodate the skill levels of all the class members.
6. Officiating should be easy, and stoppage of play should be kept at a minimum.

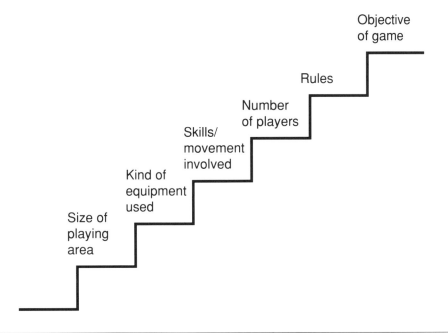

Figure 4.5 Factors that affect game structure.

7. Members of the class will not play unless teams are even.
8. The game designed can be a combination of games students already know.

Pottak (1992) distributes teaching tips for the children to use when they teach the games. After a group teaches the invented game to the rest of the class, each child completes a written evaluation of the game. The games the children invented were combination games, such as bowling and basketball skills, were diagrammed clearly, and were planned for the entire class. This is one way to focus on children inventing games.

Organizing Games to Maximize Learning

The ways in which teachers plan and manage the games can profoundly affect how children perform and what children learn in games. I waited until now to discuss organization of equipment, students, time, and space, because management only makes sense in relation to the rationale one adopts. Talking about management first would emphasize technical aspects rather than content aspects, discipline rather than the rationale for developing good games players.

However, the best intentions in teaching can be ruined if management is weak, or if management and organization are not congruent with one's beliefs about teaching, about children, and about the content (in this case, games content). Management and organization are discussed at length in a number of books, including Graham (1992), Rink (1985, 1992), and Siedentop (1991). Rather than repeat their many helpful ideas, I will discuss several concerns I have about management, especially the relationship between management and teaching. Management should *not* be considered separate from other aspects.

Organization Should Relate to Future Game Play

Practice conditions should be as much like the game requirements as possible. This does *not* mean using large groups and emphasizing game speed and accuracy; it means that the skills and strategies being learned should be used in a form approximate to real game play. This motor learning principle is easily understood with athletic teams, but it is often overlooked in physical education.

When one selects a prestructured game or combination skill practice, the organization of the game can facilitate future game play. For example, practicing basketball passes while both players slide back and forth may be a good warm-up drill, but its organization does not transfer to game play. Having 1 child in the middle of a circle pass and receive while 4 to 6 children run clockwise on the circle is *not* used in games; it also promotes dizziness.

Even when we focus on learning and combining skills, it is helpful to use an organizational pattern that can be used later in a game. Many organizational patterns would be discarded or modified if teachers "thought forward" when combining skills or teaching beginning game strategies. Before using a game, ask yourself if some approximation of this skill will be useful in games.

To learn simple game strategies, players must position and move much of the time. And they must move in a way that will be advantageous to later game play. Playing keep-away with catchers stationary is beneficial in early game instruction, but as children gain experience, they need to learn to move to receive a pass and to move after passing; these skills are essential to becoming a better games player. We need to constantly look for ways to organize space and to improve the movement of players in simplex games. If all of us do so, many games would no longer be taught in elementary programs.

Player Formations Need Careful Consideration

Traditionally, teachers have specified the organization of space and the players within the space. As we have already seen, this might interfere with students' learning to decide what to do about area of space and the relationships with teammates. This can limit children's understanding of game factors and their subsequent inventing of games. But several other problems are associated with organizations and formations.

Formations have been used to simplify where children should be and even to restrict where they can move. Formations can look good, but they cover up inadequacies in content and in learning. Formations of lines and circles indicate that the teacher is organized. A visitor with little knowledge of physical education can understand the organization and what is going on. What is often masked is the high waiting time, few turns for each child, and irrelevant structure of the activity. Relays are an excellent example. Dribbling to the end of the gym and turning around and returning to the line looks organized, but this activity has little or no content that is useful in later game play.

Relays also have other drawbacks, which I discussed earlier. Relays are not games but a type of formation. Schwager (1992) considers relays time wasters, and Williams (1992) includes relays in his list of activities in the physical education Hall of Shame. Graham (1992) cautions that relays should be used sparingly, if at all, in elementary programs.

After planning a game, selecting strategies, and considering factors that can affect games (and the criteria in this chapter), teachers should review the organization of space, players, and equipment. Table 4.3 lists questions teachers need to ask themselves, including five questions about organization.

Progress From Static to Dynamic Situations

One final idea needs to be included in organization—the players' progression in practice from being stationary to moving (Graham, 1992, pp. 103-104). The progression sequence for skill practice begins with partners stationary, working in partner-space with little space between them. For example, this can and should involve reaching to catch lead passes at different heights, directions, and arcs. Next, 1 partner is stationary and the other moves to catch. Speed, distance, and skill extensions are added. Then both partners move, perhaps slowly at first. Thus, the progression is from static (stationary) to dynamic (moving) as Graham (1992) recommends.

This same progression is needed in game play. The stationary positioning can be used when children begin to apply skills to tasks. When the number of children is increased and game play deteriorates, some of the children can be assigned (or better yet decide to have) stationary

---

Table 4.3 Questions I Need to Ask Myself

Will offense and defense have success?

Does this game reinforce and teach needed strategies?

What are the prerequisite skills and strategies for this game?

Do the students know the prerequisite strategies?

Do the children have sufficient skill in the prerequisites?

Have I planned for appropriate equipment?

Is this equipment available and ready to use?

What is sufficient space to play this game?

Do we have sufficient space to play this game safely? If not, what do I do?

What is the optimal size group for this game?

roles part of the time. In many tag, invasion, and fielding games, it is essential that children move to position, reposition, and make transitions quickly and repeatedly. The goal of game play is to move and move fast in relation to an object and what the other players are doing. If children do not possess the prerequisite skills or do not know enough strategy concepts to do this, they may benefit from simpler extensions in movement. If not, a simpler version of the game is recommended. If that doesn't work, practice in Stage 2 combination skill work is needed, at least for a short time, to reinforce the skill use.

Summary

Guidelines can be useful in planning and evaluating an elementary physical education program. Recent position statements from AAHPERD groups have been incorporated into a list of principles for developing movement programs for children. Games stages and developmental knowledge are cornerstones for devising exemplary curricula. Such programs demonstrate sequence in games instruction, characterized by partner to small-group games rather than total-class game competition.

Specific criteria can be used to select prestructured games, as well as to modify and create games. Children need to understand game factors that affect how games are played. Children can use knowledge of how games are structured to comprehend what games really are, as opposed to just learning to play a number of games. A child-centered, problem-solving teaching methodology is recommended to achieve progress in analyzing and changing games.

Teachers need to scrutinize their organization of content, as well as organization of children, for congruency and relationship to actual game play. Sound organization of games results in better progression toward game objectives and optimal participation for children.

Chapter 5

Assessing Children's Progress in Games

"One has to know where one is going, be able to carry out a plan to get there, and know when one has gotten there" (Melograno, 1979, p. xi). This statement implies that one has a rationale for where he or she is going and objectives to achieve (see chapters 1 through 4). The examples in chapters 6 through 10 illustrate the method to get to the intended destination with a degree of precision. Determining progress along the way, achieving objectives, and reaching the goal means one thing: assessment. Without assessment, one never knows how much progress has been made. With today's increased emphasis on accountability, appropriate and accurate assessment is essential.

Assessment must also be authentic (Graham, 1992). Assessment causes problems and can be a nuisance. But it is essential if one wants to know if where one is headed is where one wants to go. The problems with assessment concern at least three aspects: time, usefulness, and value. Assessment should not require an unreasonable amount of time, whether that be time to (a) administer the assessment, (b) compile and interpret the data (numbers, written statements, or other data), or (c) communicate the results (in reports, letters to or conferences with parents, or in meetings with an agency or group).

A second problem is whether assessment actually measures what one would like to have measured. Does the assessment provide useful information? Does it provide helpful feedback? Will the assessment result in an improved program? Is the assessment realistic (Werner, 1994)? This second assessment problem is entangled with the third problem, which is whether assessment is valued by the person who does the assessing. The teacher might not know what to assess or how to do it. This problem can be overcome; the assessment ideas in this and the four companion books can help. Or the teacher may be inept or not care; if that is the case, not much can help. Assessment may be difficult because of time feasibility, accuracy, and usefulness of instruments selected, but it is important to determine improvement or progress and to validate planning and teaching. The following are ideas that I have used, observed other teachers using, or designed to be realistic assessments.

Assess One Element at a Time

I'm always interested in ways to assess skills and strategies *during* actual teaching. Graham (1992) suggests observing one component at a time rather than watching a performance and picking out errors. Recently I observed a teacher say, "Now, I'm going to watch for lead passes thrown 2 to 3 feet to the side of a ready catcher."

She then gave specific verbal feedback to reinforce that aspect of the movement. She was able to pinpoint this process aspect and also relate what she observed to the total performance.

The same approach can be used for game strategies. For instance, a teacher might focus on quick changes of direction for the offense and give feedback each time that behavior was observed. Picking one strategy—like defensive positioning to clog an easy passing lane, repositioning after passing, or dropping back to support a teammate— may increase the likelihood that students attend to that strategy. All too often, what was practiced in skill work disappears in game play. I wonder if it is because teachers do not focus the children's attention on an appropriate strategy for that game. In the skill lesson I observed, the teacher, Janet Frederick, selected a skill component and counted how many times she observed that component in a specified time period. Why not do the same with a particular strategy? If the number of instances of that skill or strategy increases in subsequent lessons, that could indicate that the strategy is being applied more often, and thus better game playing is occurring— provided that the defense (or offense) did not deteriorate or just allow that strategy to happen more frequently.

Take Stats

It may also be helpful to record other behaviors during game play. Injured or excused children, children who are waiting to play (because of space limitations), or helpers can easily record such data. Using a digital stopwatch, a student could record elapsed time and the actual time a designated player possesses the ball. Even more precise assessment could be done with 2 children, each with a stopwatch. One can record the time that one team has the ball, and another can record the time a specified child has the ball. This information could be useful in helping a child understand that he or she had the ball a disproportionate amount of time or in helping a group evaluate that there was improvement in sharing the ball.

If measuring time is not feasible, taking stats like those used in competitive sports might be enjoyable and useful. I once suggested that teaching is like coaching in that both teaching behaviors and coaching behaviors could be evaluated (Belka, 1978). Player behavior can also be evaluated. Counting the number of dribbles before students pass can help in assessing whether

the children are using the priority sequence (shoot if open, pass to a player in better position, dribble to advance). In subsequent lessons, the students' goal would be to have fewer *dribble to advances*. The priority sequence can be recorded on a chalkboard or poster with the scores so the children can see the group's assessment.

Choose a strategy that is important and has been taught. (It won't work if the strategy has been mentioned only briefly or taught immediately prior to use in a large-group game.) Devise a simple score sheet to determine how many times the defensive or offensive team uses that strategy in a specified time. Repeat the same assessment in a subsequent lesson and compare the data. If the data show an increase in the use of that strategy, you have evidence that game play is improving. If the number of 2- and 3-hits in volleyball increases and the number of 1-hits decreases, you have evidence that more teammates are being used in each possession. There are many other examples of using these simple stats. Determine the skills or strategies that are important, devise a way to count how many times they occur in a game, and compare these data to data from a subsequent game.

Process Assessment

A checklist of the vital components of a skill or combination of skills can be useful. Werner (1994) has provided process checklists for use with the entire class for rolling skills and for the cartwheel. Process checklists can be designed for single and combination manipulation skills. Figure 5.1 illustrates process assessment for lead passes.

The teacher can also use process checklists to ask children to think about what they achieved in that day's lesson, for combination skills and for strategy. This can be done at the end of class when the main ideas of the lesson are reviewed. After the lesson the teacher can determine what percentage of the class made acceptable progress toward learning the main ideas.

This same procedure can be used to assess beginning offensive and defensive strategies. The main strategies can be designed by looking at the objectives for a particular game. In Advance and Score, for example, two possible offensive strategies are (a) to move without the ball to get the defender out of position and (b) to hold and move the ball to entice a defender to move closer and then pass to open teammates. Two important

Process Assessment of Skill

An important part of teaching is giving children specific feedback that is corrective, reinforcing, and congruent. This form can be used to assess a child's skill performance. The assessor observes the child for a period of time and marks the box that most accurately describes the performance.

Name _____ *Susie Learner* _____   Date _____ *June 3* _____

Skill _____ *Lead passes* _____	Almost always	Most of the time	Sometimes	Seldom
The passer				
Sends passes so that the receiver has to reach to catch				
To a stationary partner	X			
To a moving partner		X		
Sends catchable passes		X		
Sends passes to chest level				
To stationary partner	X			
To moving partner			X	
Adjusts lead to receiver's speed			X	
Leads well off a dribble				
To stationary partner	X			
To moving partner		X		
Leads well immediately after receiving a pass				
While stationary		X		
While moving			X	

Comments

Sue has consistent skills that have improved considerably in this past year. She has a tendency to avoid stopping to receive a pass or to dribble when she receives a pass while she is moving. In both cases, she doesn't look much for teammates who are open. We need to discuss this and have her set a goal for this skill.

Figure 5.1   Sample process assessment of skill in lead passes.

defensive strategies are (a) to position defensively to block the offensive progress and (b) to use fakes and move to cut off passes. The teacher or the students can use these four strategies to assess the lesson. Based on the assessment, the teacher may decide to plan extensions for the next lesson, adjust subsequent instruction for individuals, change the size of the groups, or record strategy progress. Examples of criteria to use in assessing performance in a game are shown in Figure 5.2 for Over and Under (a net game). It might also be useful to have the children devise such evaluation questions for prestructured games or for games that they design themselves.

Individual Assessment

To overlearn motor skills, children need many, many learning attempts, or turns. Figure 5.1 is an example of process assessment of a skill.

Game play can also be assessed this way. Initial attempts at any specific strategy are typically unsuccessful. Some assessment of individuals and groups is necessary to provide feedback. The assessor could consider the number of turns or chances to use a particular strategy, the quality of performance, and the success rate.

The assessment procedure can be modified to provide information about the quality of the learning chances. Rather than simply counting the number of attempts, the assessor could use a code letter corresponding to the quality of each attempt: for example, successful (S), partially successful (PS), improved (I), or unsuccessful (U). A child or an adult can count learning attempts. The data could also include turns per minute of play and percentage of improved or successful attempts. Assessing the quality of game play requires some training. The assessor must know what to look for and be able to observe the behavior during skill practice or game play. I have

Game Assessment

This is a sample assessment of one third-grade class's performance on the net game Over and Under. These items can also be used to assess individual performance.

Class _____ *Mrs. Johnson* _____   Date _____ *Oct. 20* _____

	Percentage of students who consistently perform the aspect
A. Catchers	
Move and set up well in preparation to catch	*60*
Move under or appropriately to catch bounced balls	*70*
Catch balls within their skill level	*90*
Know where to go to serve a ball	*25*
Reposition after a catch in advantageous spaces	*50*
Communicate if a ball approaches between partners	*10*
Use appropriate ready positions when time permits	*75*
B. Throwers	
Plan to throw to an unguarded area	*40*
Avoid throwing the ball too high	*30*
Reposition after a throw to a good place	*50*
Use fakes well	*40*
Throw the ball from where they catch it	*75*

C. Other tasks

Align to meet the ball in the center of body

D. Comments

I need to observe carefully to decide if the net height is too high for their throwing strength level. If so, I could lower the net or use a lighter ball. Some practice in aligning to meet the ball is needed for about 40% of the class.

Figure 5.2   Sample assessment of performance in a net game.

included such peer coaching in some games examples. Redden (1992) advocates this, also. Children who must wait because of lack of space can be assigned such assessment tasks. Learning to observe and record accurately is a lengthy process, but it is worth the effort. Other possible observers include volunteer parents, older children, or other family members. Analysis from videotape is another alternative. Figure 5.3 is a sample assessment of learning attempts.

Written Response Assessments

Children need to know how skills are performed, including important process and form aspects. In addition, knowing strategies and how to use them is vital in learning to be a games player. Having students answer questions about skill performance and strategy is one way to assess cognitive knowledge. Because most elementary

programs do not use the traditional A-B-C grading, I will call these written sets of questions *assessments* (rather than *tests*). There are many ways to use assessments. One is to administer these as Werner (1994) suggests: Design 5 to 10 multiple-choice and true-false questions to be administered at the beginning or end of class—or during class at a station to which the children would rotate. I like the station idea, especially if space is limited.

There are several other ways to conduct written or oral assessments of cognitive knowledge. One is to have partners discuss and answer the questions in a shared assessment. (If the purpose is to learn, discussion prior to answering the questions might be beneficial.) Another way would be to assign one or two completion questions as homework. It could be a way to include parents in discussing and helping the children answer the questions. Or the children could explain to the parents why a particular strategy works. The classroom teacher can be helpful in

Assessment for Skill Performance or Strategy Use

Use this to assess individual or group attempts at learning a skill or strategy.
Label each attempt as successful (S), partially successful (PS), improved (I), or unsuccessful (U). The following sample assesses how well a group of 3 students did at using a particular strategy.

Game type description _____ *3-on-2 basketball* _____

Strategies _____ *Looking for a shot or an open teammate to pass to before dribbling* _____

Student's or group's name _____ *Fifth-grade class* _____ Date __ *12/7/93* __

Number of students (group, team) ____ *3* ____ Length of time ____ *5 minutes* ____

Task 1: _____ *Passing to an open teammate closer to the goal and in a better offensive position* _____

Attempts at Task 1: _____ *S S U S S U S S U U U S S S S* _____

Turns per minute: Determine by dividing the time into the number of attempts.

15 ÷ 5 = 3.0

Success rate: Determine by dividing the number of successful attempts by the total attempts.

Today's success rate is 67%.

Two of three times a person was open, Kaitlin passed the ball. Success was interpreted as passing the ball even if the pass was errant. The decision to pass was the objective today.

Comments:

This is a significant improvement over performance from earlier this month.

If sufficient practice attempts, what is next?

To pass more accurately and continue to look for open players.

If not sufficient practice attempts to promote learning, what is needed?

For Kaitlin, Antwaun, and especially Aaron, continued emphasis on looking for teammates before dribbling

Figure 5.3   Sample assessment of a group's learning attempts at a specific skill or strategy.

distributing and collecting the papers. Also, the classroom teacher could build on a question or use the question as the basis for a writing assignment. Open-ended questions can be good assessment tools. For example, have the children write about strategies that worked and why, which strategies were difficult to use, or why some strategies were used infrequently. If the classroom teachers planned occasional short writing assignments about game play immediately after physical education class, correlation of game play and writing might be enhanced.

These ideas needn't be used every day, or even on a regular basis, but some assessment of knowledge of strategies is needed. Checklists or open-ended questions can also be used to provide feedback about children's understanding of games and how they are structured. Answers to "What I would do to improve the game is . . ." could be helpful. Other similar open-ended statements include "This game worked because . . ." and "Game play improved because . . ." Sample

questions about strategies in net or wall games are presented in Figure 5.4.

Videotaping

Although videotapes are extremely valuable in analyzing skill performance, their value in schools for assessing game progress has not been emphasized enough. Videotapes can be helpful in evaluating the lesson to determine which strategies are being used, how teammates are working together, and how children are learning to make game decisions. It's difficult to construct live simulations of strategies, but it should be easy to find a live action segment of successful defensive and offensive play to use either for instruction or evaluation of game play. Parents or grandparents may readily volunteer as camera staff. Videotaping to assess skill and game play has many possibilities for use in elementary programs.

Strategy Questions for Net and Wall Games

The following true-false items can be used to assess students' knowledge of strategy in net and wall games.

1. Hitting to an opponent's weakness is unsportspersonlike. *[False.]*
2. You should change your position to provide support for a teammate who is receiving a volley-ball. *[True.]*
3. A good strategy is to serve or send balls very high over the net. *[False; it gives the opponents extra time.]*
4. It is very important to create space in both net games and invasion games. *[True.]*
5. It is not a good idea to use fakes in net games. *[False; very useful.]*
6. You should change the way you serve so that the receiver has trouble predicting what you will do. *[True.]*
7. Hitting directly at an opponent is a poor strategy. *[False; it can cause the opponent to be crowded.]*
8. A good strategy is to hit to the open areas in your opponent's space. *[True.]*

Figure 5.4   Sample questions to assess knowledge of net and wall game strategies.

Children's Self-Assessment

Elementary children are not always accurate in judging their own performance, comparing their performance to others, setting realistic goals, and evaluating others. But with practice and gentle teacher guidance, children can become more accurate at self-assessment. The target games or application tasks can be assessed quite easily by partners (Graham, 1992). These scores are used as self-testing assessments rather than for grading or for making comparisons with other children to determine a winner. It might be useful to periodically collect these scores using individual score sheets and keep them for later comparisons for that child or set of partners. These can help in determining whether there is sufficient skill and speed to move to a more difficult task. Teachers delight when children make comments like "We had 8 in a row, didn't we?" or "Yes, let's keep going and try to get 10!" or "Let's go; we'll try forever to break our record."

Figure 5.5 shows self-assessment items for using strategy in game play. A Likert scale is used. Many scales use words like *excellent, good, fair*. The problem with such scales is that there is no clear definition for the points of the scale. Each person defines the scale individually. The scale points in Figure 5.5 are defined to reduce this interpretation problem. Other Likert scales can be devised, but the points of the scale must be defined as precisely as possible.

A self-assessment scale could be completed in successive years during the intermediate grades to provide a longer term evaluation of game play. It might be interesting for children to explain why a certain item has changed dramatically.

No discussion of evaluation about games would be complete without mentioning assessment of the affective domain. Many visual images are elicited just by mentioning affective outcomes and games. Some assessments in the affective domain should be self-assessments. These focus on whether individuals rated themselves as fair players, cooperative players, accepting of others' feelings and opinions, contributing to their group's performance, celebrating one's own success without going too far, and other feelings associated with game play. Children could use a smiley, neutral, or frowny face in their self-assessments (Graham, 1992). Or a Likert scale could be used. A sentence completion can be used to get at a particular affective aspect. Also, a self-assessment, using the Likert scale in Figure 5.5, can be designed to focus on feelings, values, or other affective concerns (see Figure 5.6).

Teacher's Self-Assessment

Graham (1992) discusses teacher self-assessment in a number of ways, at least indirectly. A few ideas will be presented here. Teachers can, and should, develop their own self-assessments based on what they are trying to accomplish. Criteria to consider include the following: Do lessons focus on the most important objectives? Do children receive sufficient quantity and quality of

Invasion Games Self-Assessment

Read each item. Circle the number that best describes your ability to use each strategy. (You can use this same evaluation some time later in the year, too.)

Name _____ *Dirk B.* _____   Date _____ *May 7* _____

Evaluative scale

4 = I use this strategy almost all the time (9 out of 10 times).
3 = I use this strategy most of the time (6-8 out of 10 times).
2 = I use this strategy some of the time (4-5 out of 10 times).
1 = I only use this strategy a few times (1-3 out of 10 times).
0 = I never use this strategy (0 out of 10 times).

Basic strategy ideas

1. I pass to open teammates.   4 3 2 1 0
2. I move to get open.   4 3 2 1 0
3. My defensive ready position is good.   4 3 2 1 0
4. I change how I play defense against an opponent.   4 3 2 1 0
5. I guard the player I am assigned to guard.   4 3 2 1 0
6. As a general rule, I position myself between the person I am guarding
    and the goal.   4 3 2 1 0
7. I know where the ball is and am ready to catch it on offense.   4 3 2 1 0
8. I try to use distance to space well on offense.   4 3 2 1 0
9. I use fakes well so my opponents do not know what I will do.   4 3 2 1 0
10. I know where the person I'm guarding is and where the ball is.   4 3 2 1 0

My best skills and strategies are _____

I need to improve on _____

Figure 5.5 Sample self-assessment items for basic invasion game strategy.

turns? Does the teacher give appropriate feedback to the children? Is the feedback congruent with the content presented?

Remembering the one or two most important objectives of the lesson can help the teacher think about the central focus of the lesson. This may be easier in skill instruction than in games instruction because games involve groups, strategies, and feelings.

Often teachers are so intent on teaching the rules of the game (e.g., soccer or football) that the rules become the central focus. The rules become more important than skill performance, and learning to use strategy takes a back seat—or is locked in the trunk of the car. If a teacher realizes that the children's performance is adversely affected by the rules, either the game is too controlled by rules or the students need simpler and fewer rules. Allowing rules to control the game is an easy trap to fall into.

Self-assessment should also consider whether the children received a sufficient number of turns to solidify skill or strategy learning. The quality

of the turns is important, too, as Graham (1992) stresses.

Related to both content focus and to quantity and quality of turns is teacher use of feedback. Graham (1992, pp. 117-125) gives useful ways to provide helpful feedback to children, especially using specific feedback. Besides providing feedback to help students correct performance, teachers need to notice and comment when children perform well. Reinforcement feedback is powerful when given appropriately, especially to beginners, who need to know when they have done something correctly. Analyzing verbal feedback for specific statements can help a teacher determine if there is the proper balance between corrective and reinforcing feedback.

Graham (1992) also stresses the need to determine how congruent feedback is with the content presented, especially the most recent content emphasis. Feedback is congruent with the content presented if the teacher has planned appropriately, observed for one or two crucial performance aspects, and then provided feedback

Feelings and Emotions

Like many activities, games cause people to feel certain things, say things, believe things, and behave in a number of ways. This form allows you to rate how you act when you play games, as well as some of your feelings when you play games. Use the following rating scale.

Evaluative scale

4 = I almost always am like this (9 out of 10 times).
3 = I am like this most of the time (6-8 out of 10 times).
2 = I am like this sometimes (4-5 out of 10 times).
1 = I am hardly ever like this (1-3 out of 10 times).
0 = I am never like this (0 out of 10 times).

1. I do my part to help the team do well and be successful.	4	3	2	1	0
2. I am considerate of others' ability levels. I never yell and get mad at them when they don't do something correctly.	4	3	2	1	0
3. I celebrate my own and my team's successes appropriately. I am a good winner.	4	3	2	1	0
4. I can lose without being angry and showing anger toward others. I am a good loser.	4	3	2	1	0
5. I play within the rules, even when no one else is watching.	4	3	2	1	0
6. I am fair to others.	4	3	2	1	0
7. I cooperate well with others.	4	3	2	1	0
8. I am willing to referee myself and tell others when I have broken a rule, such as traveling in basketball or using my hands in soccer.	4	3	2	1	0
9. I am considerate of the referee when there is one. I don't talk back and get angry at the referee.	4	3	2	1	0
10. I enjoy being a part of a team.	4	3	2	1	0

Figure 5.6   Sample self-assessment of social and emotional behavior.

about the content emphasis. In skill learning, once we write down or explain the main teaching points, it is easy to determine congruency. Of course, feedback on other performance aspects may be helpful to the learner. But, if feedback is consistently incongruent with content, the teacher may have a planning, observation, or decision problem.

Many teachers provide congruent feedback on one to three main performance points when teaching skills. The same congruency may not be as evident in games that emphasize strategy use rather than skill learning. Or there may be overemphasis on rules, as mentioned earlier. Congruency of feedback with the one to three main content emphases in *strategy* assures that one is really focusing on strategy, not on rules or skill performance. This congruency is essential to Stage 3 games instruction.

Game Criteria

The criteria presented in Chapter 4 and in Table 4.1 can be helpful in assessing and selecting games. In chapter 4, it was suggested that each

question be answered *yes* or *no* and games with many *no*s be eliminated, those with with some *no*s be modified, and those with mostly or all *yes*es be selected. The example in Figure 5.7 uses a 5-point scale and allows room for a teacher to write changes that would allow the game to be selected. Begin with a description of the game; assess the game; and determine whether the game can be played as is, needs to be modified and how it will be modified, or needs to be discarded.

Summary

Accountability requires assessing progress during instruction, as well as outcomes of the instructional program. Assessment must be feasible and valuable in terms of time and usefulness. This chapter has described a variety of assessment ideas that are easy to use and inexpensive but still provide authentic and realistic evaluation. Ideas include assessing both process and products for psychomotor, cognitive, and affective areas for both individuals and groups. The chapter also describes self-assessments for students and teachers.

Assessment Criteria for Games

Use this chart to help select and assess games. For each criteria, circle the number that best describes the game. Select games that have many items rated as important or very important. Modify games with high-numbered scores. Discard games in which many items are rated as dubious or of no value. The following example assesses the game Hoop Toss.

Name and description of game: _____ *Hoop Toss* _____

Do children possess the necessary prerequisites? ___ *Yes* ___

Scale

1 = Very important   3 = Some value   5 = No value
2 = Important   4 = Dubious value   6 = Not applicable

Criteria	Rating	Scale					
Allows maximum participation	1	1	2	3	4	5	6
Provides many quality turns	1	1	2	3	4	5	6
Is safe	2	1	2	3	4	5	6
Focuses on skills or strategy	1	1	2	3	4	5	6
Supports a developmental principle	6	1	2	3	4	5	6
Encourages efficient/effective movement	2	1	2	3	4	5	6
Builds on previous learning		1	2	3	4	5	6
Skills	1	1	2	3	4	5	6
Concepts	1	1	2	3	4	5	6
Strategy	1	1	2	3	4	5	6
Helps children become better games players	1	1	2	3	4	5	6
Enhances social and emotional status	3	1	2	3	4	5	6
Promotes consideration of individual, differing abilities	2	1	2	3	4	5	6
Others _____		1	2	3	4	5	6
_____		1	2	3	4	5	6

What changes are needed to make this game acceptable? _____ *None* _____

Figure 5.7 Example of assessment criteria used to select games.

Part II

Teaching Developmentally Appropriate Learning Experiences in Games

The second part of the book includes several chapters that describe in detail how the content might be developed for teaching children. Each chapter consists of a number of learning experiences (LEs) from which lessons can be developed. From each LE, for example, you might be able to develop two or more lessons, depending on your teaching situation. It is important to realize, however, that in many instances if one were to teach an entire LE as a lesson, the children would no doubt finish confused—and probably frustrated—because LEs contain far more than can be reasonably taught, and learned, in one 30-minute experience. Most LEs contain several objectives. For most lessons you will want to select one, maybe two, objectives to concentrate on. In other words, you want to pick a "learnable piece" that children can truly understand and grasp—rather than simply exposing them to ideas that can't be understood, let alone learned, in the time allotted.

The learning experiences in Part II are organized according to a similar format. This format is as follows:

- The *Name* of the learning experience
- *Prerequisites*, or skills (if appropriate), children should have already met in order to be

the most successful with the learning experience

- *Objectives* that explain the psychomotor, cognitive, and affective skills children will improve as a result of participating in this learning experience. When appropriate, the NASPE benchmarks that these objectives are helping students meet are referenced at the end of an objective in parentheses. The first character refers to the grade level the benchmark is found under in the official NASPE document, and the second gives the number of the benchmark itself.
- A *Suggested Grade Range* for the learning experience
- The *Organization* that children will be working in during the learning experience
- The kinds and amounts of *Equipment Needed* for presenting this learning experience to children
- A *Description* of the total learning experience, explained as if the physical education teacher was actually presenting the learning experience to children (additional information for teachers is set off in brackets)
- *Look For*, which gives key points for teachers to keep in mind when informally observing

49

children's progress in the learning experience. These are related to the objectives for the LE.

- *How Can I Change This?*, which allows you to either increase or decrease the difficulty level of the learning experience, thus allowing for all students to be challenged at their ability levels
- *Teachable Moments*, those perfect opportunities either during or after a lesson to discuss how a cognitive or affective concept is related to what has occurred in the learning experience

The next five chapters of sample learning experiences are what teachers really want to know. But without the ideas in previous chapters, these examples would be little more than things to do (Logsdon et al., 1984). Previous chapters allow us to determine if the games examples adhere to a plan and are consistent with what children can use to become better at strategy during games. I designed these examples to show more congruency with what was promised (chapters 1 to 5) than does much of the previous literature on children's games.

Example learning experiences are given for the five categories of games: chapters 6, 7, and 8 present tag, target, and net and wall games, respectively. Chapter 9 has seven invasion games, which are extremely popular with children, and chapter 10 presents four learning experiences for fielding games. I have tried, at least within each category, to put the games in order of difficulty. Although this may not always be apparent, earlier games are simpler than the following ones in the chapter.

Chapter 6

Learning Experiences for Tag Games

Four learning experiences for tag games are included in this chapter. To be included in this category, a tag game must (a) teach concepts of balance, quick changes of direction, and awareness in all directions or (b) emphasize strategies for becoming a better tag game player. Line games, circle games, and simple It games should *not* be included unless they meet one or both of these objectives. Besides having a high waiting time and no specific objectives, many traditional tag games emphasize fun instead of a movement skill or concept. Much of the time traditionally allotted for line and circle games has been shifted to educational gymnastics (Werner, 1994), educational dance (Purcell, 1994), or practice with single or combination movement skills.

Focus	Name	Suggested grade range
Copying and contrasting movements; faking; changing directions quickly	This Way and That Way	1-2
Dodging and faking	Partner Tag	3-4
Changing directions quickly	Merry-Go-Round	4-6
Changing body positions and directions with balance	Fake and Take	4-6

THIS WAY AND THAT WAY

Prerequisite

- Skill in copying a partner's body positions while the partner is stationary and some experience when the partner is moving

Objectives

As a result of participating in this learning experience, children will improve their ability to

- Change directions quickly in response to a partner's move
- Copy and contrast movement to a partner's movement
- Fake in a variety of ways

Suggested Grade Range

Primary (1-2)

Organization

Scattered in the available area

Equipment Needed

None

Description

"Today we're going to see how good of a copycat you are. You have 5 seconds to find a personal space. Go. 5, 4, 3, 2, 1. Good. Watch me carefully. I am going to run and stop. [Teacher demonstrates.] Now see if you can do that exactly the way I did it. [Demonstrate several different sequences of movement, and after each demonstration have the students mimic the movement.] Now, I'd like you to move *while* I move, but this time change direction when I do and move at the speed I do. Can you do that? I think so, too. I'll face away from you so that we'll all be moving in the same direction. [Move at slow to medium speed, change direction occasionally, and make frequent stops; add speed changes as the children react.]

"Since you're so good at this, let's try stopping in different shapes. Now you'll really have to watch me. Also, be careful to avoid others' space. [Move and stop in various shapes, including the ready position with feet shoulder-width apart, knees bent, and back almost vertical; have children imitate.]

[After several tries.] "Stop. Now I'm going to pretend that I am going to go in one direction, but then I may go another way. Let's practice this for a while. [Children practice copying teacher's movements.] Now, let's make this harder. You do the opposite of what I do. If I go fast, you go slow; if I go forward, you go backward. We won't move very far until you get the hang of it. [Move; children do opposite.]

"This time, let's pretend that you have to get away from your shadow. When you move, quickly lean one way, then move in the other direction. Try this right now in your personal space. Move one body part one way, then quickly change its direction. Use new and different body parts to start with each time. Go. [Call out the names of body parts children use without stopping the class.] Stop. Let's watch Jerry and Allison pretend to go one way but then go the other. [Pinpoint both students.] Jerry and Allison are *faking*—they are trying to make their shadows go one way and then they go the other way. Now, you use different body parts to try to fake your shadow. Go this way and that way. Ready, go. [Give feedback.] Good. I see some of you leaning your head one way to fake. Others are using a hand. A shoulder. Oh, Miranda just leaned her whole body one way but moved the other way; the shadow had trouble keeping up.

"Stop. This time, you want to make your shadow look at a part that's not at the middle of your body. Why do you want to do that? [The parts away from the center can easily fool another person; the middle of the body, the hips, actually cause the direction change.] OK, try to fake your shadow. Go. [After several tries.] Stop. Now let's pretend the shadow is trying to fake you out. Remember, watch the center of the shadow, not the edges or outside area. Pretend that both you and your shadow are foot-dribbling or hand-dribbling. Don't be fooled by the shadow's moves to dodge you. You might even pretend that the shadow is another person. Go.

[After several tries.] "Stop. On 5, get a partner and watch me. 5, 4, 3, 2, 1. You almost made it. Are all eyes watching me? OK, here's what we're going to do. One partner will move while the other one watches. Staying in a small space, one partner moves, then stops, then moves, and stops. The mover should stay within three to four steps of the partner, who is watching. Then the watcher tries to copy the moving exactly. After you copy, then you get a chance to have your partner copy you. Try to make the moving and stopping interesting but not too hard. [Have children take several turns moving and copying; some children may begin to add shapes in stopping.] Try to stop in a definite shape. That will make it more exciting to copy.

[After some more tries and while the children are working.] "When you're ready, copy your partners *as* they move.

[After several turns.] "Now, this time go in the *opposite* direction of your partner. What body parts do you watch to know which way your partner will turn? [Center of body, hips.] What body parts can be used to trick you—to make you think the other person might go one way when they might not? [Feet, head, any one part—watch the whole body.] You have 1 minute before we're done today. Go."

Look For

- Children moving and changing directions quickly with good balance.
- Definite faking moves (ones that look real) and good balance during the faking and subsequent moving.

How Can I Change This?

- Restrict to stationary positions but allow level or height changes.
- Restrict to two to three steps or one to three movements.
- Have partners face each other and do the same task. Each needs safety space behind because one will move backward if the partner moves forward.
- If skill permits, add a manipulation task. For example, one person can dribble, while the other copies and tries to maintain a given distance. Partners can face the same direction or opposite directions.

PARTNER TAG

Prerequisite

- Ability to move through general space without interfering with others' space or movement

Objectives

As a result of participating in this learning experience, children will improve their ability to

- Keep in a balanced position while trying to dodge an opponent (3-4, #1)
- Fake using a variety of body parts
- Tag softly without getting tagged

Suggested Grade Range

Intermediate (3-4)

Organization

Pairs of children move in 10-foot squares (or smaller, if necessary) marked off with cones (see Figure 6.1).

Equipment Needed

Enough cones or markers are needed to divide space; gym floor lines could also be used.

Description

"Today we're going to see how good we are at tricking somebody. Without touching anyone, spread out inside the boundary lines. Show me a very balanced position so that you can move quickly in all directions. Are your hips high or low? [Low.] Are you more balanced if you're standing up tall or crouched? [Crouched.] Will you be able to move more quickly with your feet together or apart? [Apart but not too far.] Should your feet be straddled sideways, or forward and backward? [It depends; the forward-backward straddle is helpful for moving forward and backward; the sideward straddle

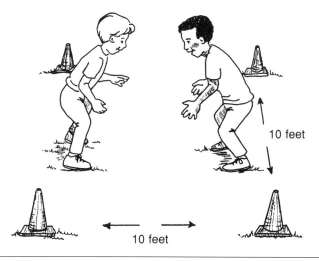

10 feet

10 feet

Figure 6.1 Partner Tag.

helps in going sideways.] Practice moving in all directions from both of these positions. Try this on your own for 20 seconds. Go! [Signal to stop.] Try it again.

"On the count of five, stand and face a partner. 5, 4, 3, 2, 1. Good, you did that quickly. Both you and your partner will be It. Inside an area about the size you see here [Demonstrate.], move and try to tag your partner but try to avoid getting tagged. Tag with a soft pat or easy touch, so you don't hurt your partner. If you get tagged, take five hops or jumps and continue the game. Give your partner 4 or 5 seconds after she or he hops or jumps to signal to start the game again. You need to try to stay very balanced and try to tag your partner when he or she is a little off-balance. The best time to tag your partner is when he or she is not in a balanced straddle position. Stop when I say stop. Get cones and make your area, position yourselves, and begin when you are ready. Go!

[After several tries.] "Stop. Before we start again, let's think about how balanced and ready we are. Are you balanced so that you can move quickly in any direction? Your legs need to be springy, with most of your weight on the balls of your feet. Show me the ball of your foot. Good. Try this good ready position where you are while you face me. I'll watch as you balance, then try to move. Go! I see knees bent and good balancing. That springy position looks very good. That means your weight is where? Right, the balls of your feet, or the front part. On your toes? On your heels? [No.] Keep working just by yourself. Try to look, nod, or move a body part one way but then move the other way. But just move one step or even part of a step—that is faking. Try it on your own. I see some people moving their heads; others are faking with the hand, the leg, shoulder—many different parts. Keep faking and moving a little longer. I'll just watch.

"Face your partner again and get in a balanced position, ready for Partner Tag. Go ahead and play. [During play, make remaining points.] Remember to tag softly. Oh, good faking with your hands, Mina. I see some of you shifting your weight one way and then moving in another direction. Good idea. Quick faking movements cause partners to move, even go off-balance just long enough for you to try to tag them."

Look For

- Children using fakes and changes of directions to keep their balance while trying to get their partners off-balance.
- Soft pat tags or touches.
- Good balanced positioning, keeping knees bent and feet straddled.

How Can I Change This?

- Make the area smaller, or increase the size of the playing area so that locomotion is involved.
- Each child has a yarn ball and tries to use an underhand toss to touch the other's foot (or another body part). This involves moving the body or a body part to avoid contact with the yarn ball.
- Have one partner screen a ball while hand- or foot-dribbling or catching, using the body as a barrier between the ball and the other partner (defender).
- Increase the group size to 3 or 4 in a bigger area. This extension involves being in a good ready position, moving the upper body to monitor all directions, and even moving the entire body during monitoring.
- Increase the group and area size, even to having the entire class playing (everyone's It).

MERRY-GO-ROUND

Prerequisites

- Ability to change direction quickly and keep one's balance
- Reasonable success playing Partner Tag

Objectives

As a result of participating in this learning experience, children will improve their ability to

- Slide and move sideways, changing directions quickly, and communicate effectively with other players
- Fake and change direction quickly

Suggested Grade Range

Intermediate (4-6)

Organization

Groups of 4 children move in 10-foot squares marked off with cones (see Figure 6.2).

Equipment Needed

Enough cones to divide space, 1 whistle (optional)

Description

"I think you will enjoy playing this game today. It's called Merry-Go-Round. Have you ever been on one? Merry-Go-Round is played in groups of 4. To play, one person is It. One person in the circle is the target that the It tries to tag. The circle must keep hands joined and move sideways so that one certain person cannot be tagged by It. The It runs left and right, changing directions, and tries to get around the outside of the circle to lightly tag the target person on the shoulder or back. Play begins on my *go* signal; when I say stop (or blow the whistle), everyone stops. If anyone slips or gets in a dangerous position, say 'Help' and your game stops immediately. This is very

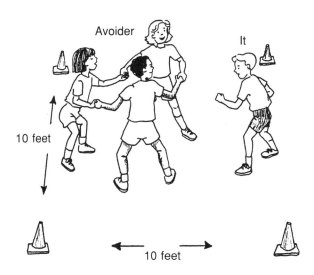

Figure 6.2   Merry-Go-Round.

important. When I say 'Go,' get into groups of 4, choose who is It and who should avoid being tagged, and get ready. You will all get turns at all roles. If the target person gets tagged before the stop signal, get ready for the next game. Go.

[During play and between turns.] "Tagger, try to force the group to stop too soon or go too far around. Circle, move as one person, not three. Work like a merry-go-round, very smoothly.

[After a number of turns, signal to stop.] "Stop! Now that we have played this, how is this game similar to Partner Tag? [Good balance, quick changes of direction, good faking are needed.] How is this game different?" [The circle children must work together and even communicate to each other what to do; sliding is the main way to move; the It must stay close to the circle people and avoid wide circular paths.]

Look For

- The It using fakes and changes of directions to keep balance while trying to get the target person to move toward the It.

- The circle players using sideward movement, preferably sliding, as a unit to position the target person away from the It.

- Circle players talking to help each other coordinate when to change directions.

How Can I Change This?

- Allow the It to tag on the upper arm or the entire arm.

- Extend the time limit. The circle players have a difficult communication task to maintain; the longer the time, the more difficult this becomes.

- Require the It to tag in the middle one third of the back or to take a belt flag from the side of the child's waist.

- Change from a circle formation to a line; players place hands on the hips of the person directly in front. The player at the back of the line is the target that the It tries to tag. Now the person at the end of the line must move considerably farther and faster than the one at the front (see Figure 6.3).

> **TEACHABLE MOMENT**
>
> Explain that this game is called Merry-Go-Round because of the smooth, unison movement involved. Moving and faking by the It causes the circle group to change direction too soon or very quickly, perhaps getting the group out of sync.

Figure 6.3   Line version of Merry-Go-Round.

FAKE AND TAKE

Prerequisites

- Skill in starting, stopping, and changing direction quickly while moving fast (If children cannot stop quickly and avoid contact with others, safety concerns might prohibit playing this game. Stress safety emphatically.)
- Skill in faking, dodging, and tagging another person
- Experience in Partner Tag and Merry-Go-Round

Objectives

As a result of participating in this learning experience, children will improve their ability to

- Adjust body position quickly with balance
- Fake and cause another person to lose balance
- Quickly react to another's movements by repositioning oneself (3-4, #1)

Suggested Grade Range

Intermediate (4-6)

Organization

Groups of 3 children play in 8-foot by 35-foot areas; 2 positioned opposite each other, each about 8 feet from a small, empty plastic detergent or 2-liter bottle, facing the bottle. The 3rd child is near the bottle but not in the others' way. A line or marker is used to indicate the starting positions of the 2 children (see Figure 6.4).

Equipment Needed

1 empty plastic detergent or 2-liter bottle for each group, floor markings or cones for starting lines

Figure 6.4   Fake and Take.

Description

"I think you will enjoy playing this game today. Let's look at Carla and Scottie. Each is standing on a line facing each other and a bottle. Bill is the helper. When Bill says 'Go,' both Carla and Scottie run up to and try to take the bottle, then run safely back past their starting line before being tagged by the other person. If you don't get the bottle, you need to react quickly and try to softly tag the person before that person is safe. Let's watch.

[After one or two attempts, comment on the play.] "Carla faked well, took the bottle, and got past the line. Scottie almost reacted fast enough to tag Carla. It's a good idea to change position, fake but be balanced, and be ready to take and go, or react and tag. On 'Start,' get into groups of 3, each group get a plastic bottle, set up so that you will not interfere with other groups, and begin play. Remember to change the helper after each time, but do it so each person gets to play against both other players. Start.

[After 6 to 10 turns.] "Stop. Everyone come on in close. Let's think about what has happened so far. When do you think is the best time to take the bottle and run? [When the other person is off-balance.] Yes, that's right. One of the worst times may be when you arrive at the bottle and stop just ahead of the other person. Why do you think that is so? [You have to slow down, stop, and change direction. If you take the bottle then, the other person is still running and will tag you.] So the best time to take the bottle is just when the other person stops. That's because the person has to shift his or her weight from the back, when they stopped, to forward again so they can chase the person who just took the bottle. You need to understand this idea because it will come up again and again in many games. Yes, Darrin, that's right. If both people get near the bottle at about the same time, the strategy changes. Now you have to fake to get the person off-balance, then try to take the bottle, which is why this game is named Fake and Take. Let's begin again, this time looking for when a person is off-balance, going from forward to backward to take the bottle. Go.

[During play.] "I see some players faking forward, backward, and even moving sideways. Nancy and Marie turned halfway so that they were facing their own starting line. That requires new strategies to be used. We'll work on those next time."

Look For

- Children deciding to take the bottle when the other child has just stopped or is shifting away from the bottle.
- Good balance positions allowing movement in a number of directions.
- Use of fakes to move the other person off-balance or conceal when one is taking the bottle.

How Can I Change This?

- Have both players begin stationary within several steps of the plastic bottle.
- Allow a player to drop the bottle if that player senses that he or she is going to be tagged. Play continues.

> **TEACHABLE MOMENT**
>
> Allow the helper to decide where to place the bottle to adjust for unequal speed of the 2 players. Discuss how this is done to make the game more fair for both players.

Chapter 7

Learning Experiences for Target Games

Unlike the other categories of games, target games are self-paced. The performer decides when to begin and how to do the skill. There usually is not a defense that could force a change of plans. Also, these games may be cooperative or competitive, depending on the skill level of the children and the objectives of the lesson. Target games are useful in testing whether children can control the skill precisely. The challenge of accuracy in controlling a skill makes target games exciting for children. Teachers can decide when to emphasize accuracy. Target activities can be modified by adjusting distance, target size, equipment, and skills required; by using stationary or moving targets; and by having performers be stationary or mobile.

Target games are application tasks (Rink, 1992) that can be part of a lesson or modified to challenge individuals within a single instructional task. Target games or activities can be modified easily for use with very young children if accuracy is not overemphasized. Children can benefit from appropriate challenges in target games throughout the year. There are hundreds of target games. Common basketball games (such as Horse and Around the World), bowling at pins, putting or golf chipping, and lawn darts or horseshoes can be useful but are not explained in this book because of space limitations. Four learning experiences are presented in this chapter, including one that involves a defender.

Focus	Name	Suggested grade range
Kicking accurately using the inside of the foot	Aim and Go!	3-4
Throwing accurately from two surfaces; catching rebounding balls	Predict a Bounce	5-6
Kicking to a goal; goalie play	Defend the Shots	5-6
Throwing Frisbees accurately	Mini-Frisbee Golf	5-6

AIM AND GO!

Prerequisite

- Some skill in kicking using the inside of the foot

Objective

As a result of participating in this learning experience, children will improve their ability to

- Kick for accuracy with the left and the right foot with emphasis on kicking with the inside of the foot

Suggested Grade Range

Intermediate (3-4)

Organization

Partners are spaced 20 to 40 feet apart (or any distance that is challenging and available) and 4 cones (or other appropriate target) are placed 10 feet apart in a square on the ground halfway between the partners. One player has the ball (see Figure 7.1).

Equipment Needed

1 foam soccer ball and 4 cones (or long jump rope or 4 hoops for target) for each group of 2

Description

"Accuracy, or sending an object exactly where we aim, is becoming more and more important in our game play. Today, we are going to work on kicking a ball. We'll try to make the ball go between the cones and then on to a partner. Watch me. [Teacher kicks a stationary ball, aiming for a target about 10-foot square about 20 feet away.

Figure 7.1 Aim and Go!

The ball rolls through the target to Sara, a student standing opposite and about 20 feet past the target.] What part of my foot made contact with the ball? That's right, the inside. Today, accuracy is more important than distance. You will need to kick with control instead of hard for distance. Remember to contact the ball at or even a little bit higher than the center of the ball, using the inside or *instep* of your foot—no toes. That will keep the ball moving along the ground, instead of high in the air.

"Did you notice that the ball was still when I kicked it? Try stopping the ball without using your arms or hands, then kicking it. Watch Sara demonstrate. [Sara then stops the ball without using her arms and hands and kicks the ball back to the teacher, trying to pass it through the target.] Pair up, get a ball, and set up a target area. Make the target area a size that will challenge you but not be too difficult. When I say 'Go,' begin. Go!

[After the children have begun kicking.] "Stop. I notice many of you are using only one foot. Try five kicks with your right foot and then five with your left foot. Move closer to or further from the target so that it is challenging but not too difficult. Receivers, remember to try many different ways of stopping and trapping the ball, without using your arms and hands. The ball needs to be stopped before you kick it through the target. Ready; begin again. [Give feedback during practice.] I like the way you are using the inside of your foot to kick the ball. You're also contacting it just above center. Good! Watch the ball very closely as you kick. Think of the target in your mind, but watch the ball during contact.

"If you choose, keep your own score. You get 1 point if you kick the ball and 2 points for kicking through the target. See how many points you get when we're done."

Look For

- Children kicking using the inside of the foot.
- Careful aiming rather than hurried kicking.
- Children offering verbal and nonverbal encouragement to partners.
- Differences in distances for partners so that individual skill abilities are better accommodated.

How Can I Change This?

- Have students try sending fly balls by contacting the ball below the center and with the instep of the foot (shoe laces); allow the kick to then bounce in and through the target area.
- Have students dribble to one side and then kick toward the target.
- See how many successes partners can achieve cooperatively. Have them work toward the best of 10 tries, the best in a specified time period, or the best in a row (or breaking their previous best record).

PREDICT A BOUNCE

Prerequisite

- Practice throwing at targets and collecting and catching rebounds off the wall

Objective

As a result of participating in this learning experience, children will improve their ability to

- Predict angles of a thrown, rebounding ball to make it land in an intended area (5-6, #1)

Suggested Grade Range

Intermediate (5-6)

Organization

Pairs or trios of children face a wall so that all groups have space to throw toward targets and retrieve rebounds. Each group is assigned an area of 10 feet by half the width of the gym (or longer if space is available). (See Figure 7.2.)

Equipment Needed

3 tennis balls (or similar bouncy balls) for each group (if space is very limited, use 3- to 5-inch rubber balls or small sponge balls); enough cones to mark target area on the floor; tape to mark targets on walls (or other adjustable markers)

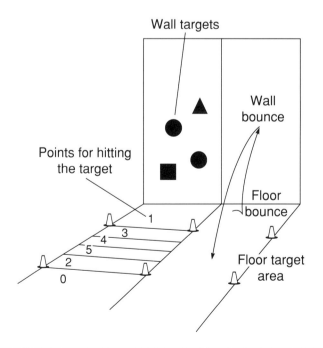

Figure 7.2   Predict a Bounce.

Description

"You're getting skilled at throwing at targets on the wall. We're going to make this harder now and ask you to be much more accurate. Your task is to bounce the ball, have it hit the wall, and then rebound into the area marked by the cones. It's like the ball ricochets off the floor and wall. Watch! [Demonstrate.] The idea is to bounce the ball on the floor, have it hit the wall, and then rebound to the target area on the floor. Each person gets three tries; keep track of how many of your throws score a point by landing in the target area. If the target area is too easy or too hard, adjust the distance of the cones to make it more challenging. Your partner will be standing near the back set of cones to catch the ball after it bounces in the target area. Remember, another group is behind you throwing to the opposite wall. Try to keep all balls in your area. When I say 'Now,' get into pairs and go to one of the areas already set up. Check the distance with other groups for safety, and begin. Now!

[After some play begins.] "Stop. If this is too difficult, choose one of the targets on the wall to have the ball rebound toward, and don't worry about where it goes on the floor for a while. You decide. If it's too easy, add a scoring system to make it harder. The sender can get 1 point for hitting the floor target and the receiver 1 point for a successful catch. Go.

[After more practice.] "Stop. You may have to adjust the pathway the ball travels in the air, or its arc, to have the ball land in the target area on the floor. To do this, you'll have to think about the force you throw the ball with and the angle at which the ball rebounds off the floor and wall. That's a lot to plan and think about. Let's begin again and really concentrate on your force and the angle of the rebounding ball. Go.

[If and when needed.] "Be considerate of others. If your ball goes into another area, wait until a throw is completed in that area, then move behind the other players to get your ball. This shows respect for others. It is also for safety."

Look For

- Relaxed throwing.

- Senders conceptualizing the angles and force required.

- Receivers moving in relation to the arc and bounce of the ball.

How Can I Change This?

- Change to floor bouncing to hit wall targets only.

- Use bigger area targets or move closer to the wall.

- Concentrate solely on the accuracy of throwing to various size targets. If rebounding is then a problem because of skill, organization, or space, use balls that do not bounce, such as yarn balls.

- Have students move in very close to the wall. In a way, this makes it easier because less accuracy is needed in the initial throw, but adjusting force to cause the needed rebound arc is challenging.

- Design floor targets with tape, markers, or cones with differing values (see the floor targets in Figure 7.2).

- Set a target at a certain wall height, and bounce the ball from the floor to rebound to hit the target. Change distances from the wall.

- Have students throw the ball off of a corner (two walls) and make it land in a target area on the floor.

TEACHABLE MOMENTS

If competition is not close, what can be done to make it more equal and challenging for all players? Solutions include choosing partners who are more equal in ability and changing target size depending on ability.

Before throwing try to see in your mind exactly how and where the ball will go. This is called making a mental image in planning.

Discuss how a ball can rebound at different angles. Show the difference between a small and narrow angle; relate this to angles in mathematics.

DEFEND THE SHOTS

Prerequisites

- Experience in trying to block shots coming low or high to either side
- Acceptable balance and footwork for defending a goal
- Some successful practice at kicking balls toward targets

Objectives

As a result of participating in this learning experience, children will improve their ability to

- Plan and execute a target kick toward a defended goal
- Defend a goal and anticipate attempts to score

Suggested Grade Range

Intermediate (5-6)

Organization

One child sets a ball on the ground 15 feet from a 10-foot goal area defended by a 2nd child. A 3rd child is on the other side of the goal to retrieve balls (see Figure 7.3).

Equipment Needed

1 or 2 foam or soft #4 balls and 1 goal net (or other goal) for each group of 3 children (This could be done inside with taped goal areas on the walls.)

Description

"Defending a free shot is different than defending during regular play. Our game today will help us defend a goal, or be a goalie. It's played in groups of 3. One player stands

Figure 7.3 Defend the Shots.

still near the ball, which is on a place marked on the ground. The 2nd player, the goalie, stands still near the middle of the goal in a good balanced position with hands ready. The goalie may not jump or let her or his feet leave the ground until the kicker touches the ball. When both players are ready, the 3rd person says 'Go' and waits to retrieve balls that get past the goalie. The kicker has about 15 seconds to plan and attempt a kick at the goal. Each kicker has three chances to score; then players change places. Be sure that everyone gets a chance to kick and defend the same number of times and that defenders get practice with both other players as kickers. On 'Go,' get with 2 other people, get equipment, set up, and begin. Go! [This assumes that the protocol (Graham, 1992) is learned so well that the children can easily decide the equipment needed, as well as space needed, in a considerate and safe manner.]

[Stop the class after a while.] "Where do you think is the best part of the goal to kick to? Yes, Brianna, the best target is in one of the corners of the goal. Why? [The corners are the most difficult areas to defend.] What can the goalie do to be a good defender? [Be balanced, with hands ready to catch; be prepared to move quickly in any direction; and watch intently to try to predict where the ball will be sent.]

"Kickers need to use fakes—with their eyes, their body parts, and by changing the amount of time they use. They need to vary their attempts so that the goalie cannot predict their kicks. Keep these in mind as you play; we'll work on them other times, too. Go!"

Look For

- Defenders who begin to read the kicker's probable target by watching where the ball is kicked to.

- Good faking by the kicker to hold the goalie in place longer or conceal the direction of the shot.

How Can I Change This?

- Increase the size of the goal to make it easier for the kicker.

- Reduce the size of the goal to make it easier for the goalie.

- Set up several balls for 2 kickers or 1 ball for 3 or more kickers. The goalie must prepare for another shot as soon as he or she plays the present shot.

- Allow the kicker to take several steps before kicking the ball (harder for the goalie).

- Goalie play can be changed to include a variety of methods to score (e.g., throwing as in team handball or striking as in field hockey).

TEACHABLE MOMENT

There may be a need to discuss fairness—when to begin and whether a particular attempt was a goal or not. The third person assumes the referee's role; the others need to respect and accept the referee's decisions.

MINI-FRISBEE GOLF

Prerequisites

- Control in throwing Frisbees in straight and curved directions
- Knowledge that release position and wrist snap cause the Frisbee to fly differently and knowing how this occurs
- Understanding that wind current affects the Frisbee and ability to adjust the throw to compensate or attempt to compensate

Objective

As a result of participating in this learning experience, children will improve their ability to

- Throw a Frisbee (or deck ring or plastic lid) for accuracy (5-6, #1)

Suggested Grade Range

Intermediate (5-6)

Organization

Partners or trios begin at different stations or target holes; 9 holes are set up in a playing area that can be either a gym or larger outside area. Students are given score cards, directions sheets, and maps; directions are posted appropriately (see Figures 7.4 and 7.5).

Equipment Needed

1 Frisbee per child; 1 score card, 1 directions sheet, 1 pencil, and 1 map of the course per group of 2 or 3 children; 18 one-gallon milk jugs; 1 small table; 2 poles; 1 barrel;

Hole #	Tee/starting area	Actual hole or target
1	Stand between #1 markers.	Land *in* red hoop on ground.
2	Between #2 markers	Land *on* small table.
3	Between #3 markers	Pass *through* yellow hoop set up vertically between two trees or poles.
4	Between #4 markers	Dogleg right around obstacles. Land *in* box.
5	Between #5 markers	Land *in* the blue hoop.
6	Between #6 markers	Land *in* the barrel.
7	Between #7 markers	Throw *through* the vertical hoop and then land *on* the card table.
8	Between #8 markers	Dogleg left around obstacles. Land *in* the wheelbarrow.
9	Between #9 markers	Land *in* the smaller white hoop after passing *through* the narrow fairway (could use standing mats, etc.).

Figure 7.4 Mini-Frisbee Golf directions.

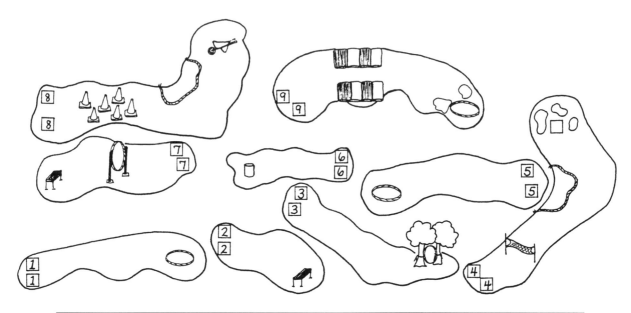

Figure 7.5   Mini-Frisbee Golf map.

1 wheelbarrow; 2 standing mats; 1 box; 5 hoops (1 red, 1 yellow, 1 blue, 1 small white, and 1 miscellaneous); 6 cones; 4 jump ropes; and 1 net. See Figure 7.5 for a possible course set-up.

Description

"You've all seen golf, haven't you? Today we're going to play a miniversion using these plastic Frisbees. We've been practicing straight and curved throwing, and you understand how to make the Frisbee curve and how wind can affect your throws. The object is to control the way you throw your Frisbee. You want to send it to various targets with the fewest throws. There are 9 holes. You'll begin between 2 plastic milk jugs. We'll call this the tee. A tee is where we begin. Notice these jugs are numbered 1. This is tee 1. Each group of 2 or 3 will have a card telling you what target, or hole, to begin at.

"Watch Chelsea and me. Each of us tosses a Frisbee toward the red hoop. We go to where our Frisbee lands. Since I am farther away, I throw next. Then Chelsea. We continue like this, trying to get the Frisbee in the red hoop. [Continue.] Then we add up the number of throws each of us takes to get *in* the hole. That is our group score. It's better to have *fewer*, than *more*, throws to a hole. Hole 2 is next and is different. We need to get the Frisbee *on* the table. Each hole is a different distance and has a different target.

"On 'Go,' get in twosomes or threesomes, each person with a Frisbee. Each group gets a score card and a little pencil. Check your card for your starting hole number. Questions? Go!

[After 9 holes.] "Add your group scores on each hole for the 9 holes. [After adding scores.] I've added all scores, and the class's total is [insert score]. Let's try another round of 9 holes, and let's try to lower the class score." [The focus on group and class aggregate scoring is considerably different than traditional scoring.]

Look For

- Students taking time to plan the force and pathway of the throws.
- Students pacing themselves so that they are not rushing and waiting for those in front to finish.

How Can I Change This?

- Use larger targets, or reduce the distance from tee to target.
- Use a heavier Frisbee (if space permits) so that wind resistance is much less of a factor.
- Use smaller targets, or increase the distance from tee to target.
- Determine what par is for each hole, and post that so that students can begin to learn golf scoring. Next teach them about over and under par.
- Compare individual scores within groups. I would recommend this *if* the students requested it and I thought they were ready for friendly competition.
- This same organization could be used for kicking a ground ball or for rolling or throwing a beanbag or foam ball for accuracy.

TEACHABLE MOMENTS

If crowding occurs, explain the need to wait for the twosome or threesome in front to have adequate time and space so that they are not hurried. This is essential if the children are using hard Frisbees. This would also be important on a golf course; it's consideration of others.

Slowly introduce golf terms as they are needed or as they come up in play. Here are some examples: round of golf—usually 9 holes of play; tee—the area designated to begin play for a specific hole; fairway—the space from the tee to near the hole; green—the smaller area around the cup or hole; cup or hole—the target for the Frisbee or golf ball.

Chapter 8

Learning Experiences for Net and Wall Games

Net and wall games are easy to conceptualize and are related to target games, which involve accuracy in hitting to a specified area. Thorpe et al. (1986) suggest that strategy in these games is easier to learn than strategy in invasion and fielding games. In many net games, single players or teams remain on one side of the net, so sharing space is easier than in invasion and keep-away games. The intricate rules, special circumstances, and strategies for particular fielding games make such games difficult to visualize. In contrast, in net games, one need only return an object across the net into an area and then move, sometimes only slightly, to cover one's space. But the skills involved and the speed of play make net and wall games challenging and difficult. Much of the time devoted to net and wall skills may be better planned for developing and combining skills rather than in competitive play. Three learning experiences are described in this section.

Focus	Name	Suggested grade range
Volleying	Across the Line	3-4
Throwing accurately; moving to catch	Over and Under	3-4
Bumping and setting, possibly serving, for accuracy	Over Long and Short	5-6
Striking with a short-handled racket for accuracy	Three-Court Tennis	5-6

ACROSS THE LINE

Prerequisite

- Practice in tapping a ball to oneself and to a partner

Objective

As a result of participating in this learning experience, children will improve their ability to

- Control a ball by tapping for easy striking or volleying it away from a partner

Suggested Grade Range

Intermediate (3-4)

Organization

Two children are positioned in a marked area 6 to 8 feet square.

Equipment Needed

1 7- to 8.5-inch rubber ball per pair; if lines are not available, use chalk or water-soluble liquid shoe polish to make lines (Long cardboard tubes or paper rolls on cones can also make a "net.")

Description

"Across the Line is a tapping, or volleying, game—not a catching game—so no catching is allowed. This will make it interesting! You try to tap or volley the ball so that it bounces inside your partner's area but does not touch the center line. Watch Missy and Angie do this. See how one of them tries to tap it directly back, making the other one move to play the ball in her area? Remember what a control tap is? No? Well, when you receive a ball, you are allowed one or two control taps so that you have time to plan where to send the ball and to use fakes before sending it. Control taps can be off the hands or off the hands with a bounce on the floor. Defenders need to position to cover the whole area. They also need to be in a balanced, ready position that permits reaching low or high, as well as moving in all directions—in case they have to go somewhere else in the area. When I say 'Go,' get a partner and a ball, and set up a play area. You may use any line on the floor, or you may set up the paper rolls on cones to make a center barrier or net. Go.

[During play.] "Send balls in upward and downward directions. Try to send the ball to where the other least expects it. Vary your sending. If you are the defender, keep balanced, even after you have turned or moved.

[After some play]. "Stop. If you want to, design your own rules and procedures. But only make a rule if it helps the game go smoothly or requires more skill, and if it is agreed upon by all players. I'll come around to see your game. Go."

Look For

- Defensive positions that are balanced and ready.
- Placing the ball away from the other person.

How Can I Change This?

- Return to partner passing for consecutive passing (a skill application but also a cooperation task).

- Change the shape of the playing area. This can change the game, at least slightly, in terms of where to play and how to tap to the other players (see Figure 8.1).
- Change to three- or foursquare.

TEACHABLE MOMENT

Discuss how people feel when they miss a ball that they think they should have caught. Would comments from others such as "That's OK" help more than comments that make fun of the person? We should all remember that when other people miss, we should try to say things that help them.

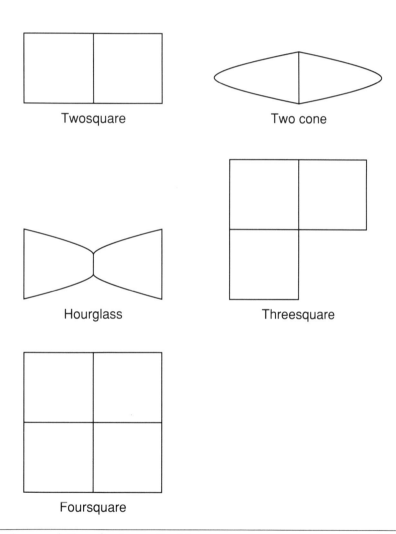

Twosquare

Two cone

Hourglass

Threesquare

Foursquare

Figure 8.1 Area variations for Across the Line.

OVER AND UNDER

Prerequisite

• Skill in catching a bouncing ball, from self or a partner, coming from various heights and angles

Objectives

As a result of participating in this learning experience, children will improve their ability to

• Throw a ball over an obstacle so that it lands in a specified area
• Move in order to catch an aerial ball

Suggested Grade Range

Intermediate (3-4)

Organization

Two children play in a 16-foot square area that is divided by a net or rope 6 to 8 feet high; each child is in an area 16 feet wide and 8 feet deep (see Figure 8.2).

Equipment Needed

1 net or rope and 1 7-inch rubber or foam ball for each pair of children. Cones, rubber disks, or tape can also be used to mark boundaries if volleyball courts are not available.

Description

"We are getting very good at throwing a ball over a rope or net, and our partners are becoming better at catching fly balls and bouncing balls by getting under the ball to catch it. Now, what would happen if we tried to throw the ball over the net and have it bounce so our partner has trouble catching it? That would really change the task,

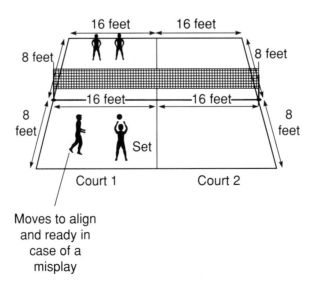

Figure 8.2 Over and Under.

wouldn't it? Let's watch Billy and Joel try this. [Explain while students demonstrate.] We have some new rules now. You have to throw the ball over the net from where you catch it, and you can't take more than one step after you catch the ball. Try to catch the ball after only one bounce; if you do this, you score a point. Keep playing until a player does not catch the ball after one bounce only *or* the ball does *not* bounce in the playing area. If these happen, stand in the middle of your area and begin a new sequence by throwing the ball over the net and bouncing it in your partner's area. This is called a *serve*. When I say 'Go,' get a partner and a ball, go to one of the net [rope] areas, and play this game. Go.

[After some practice.] "Stop. I want you to think about a good place to stand so that you'll be ready to go anywhere in the space to catch a ball. Catchers, think where the other player is most likely to send the ball; you will need to move quickly to position to catch. Throwers, think of ways to keep the other player from knowing exactly where you will send the ball. Go.

[After some time.] "Stop. Look over here. We've made the game more exciting by putting 2 players on each side. Now the 2 players will need to share the space. They'll need to talk with each other, especially for balls that are between them. The person closest or in best position needs to say 'I got it.' Partners need to be considerate; they need to let the person in better position catch the ball. Good players do that. If you want to play with 4 people, you can, or you can stay with 2. Begin again.

[During play.] "Remember, partners need to space themselves to cover *all* the space on their side of the net. Throwers, send the ball to places that will be hard to defend. Look for open areas. Fake before you throw, but you may only hold the ball for a few seconds.

[After some time, it may be useful to show several pairs and discuss their good use of center court positioning to receive, their faking on offense and defense, and their accuracy in throwing. Such pinpointing may be needed in many lessons. An example follows.]

"I see some of you passing on your own side of the net. This gets the ball to a partner who may be in better position to throw to an open space. That is smart playing." [This will likely require discussion of moving to set up to cover the whole space, especially in relation to the changing situation after a catch or after a partner pass prior to a ball being sent over the net. This could be a learning piece in which some time could be directed toward teaching coverage of the area depending on where the opponents are positioned on their side. That is to be expected. If students comprehend this easily, stay with this modification. If not, consider changing to a task that focuses more on coverage and positioning with simpler throwing and catching skills.]

Look For

- Throws that are no higher than required to send the ball where it was intended to go (i.e., balls that are too high may allow the defender too much time to set up).
- Catchers moving so that they are aligned to catch the ball near the midline of the body and to send it back in a number of directions. This is a prerequsite skill for games such as volleyball.
- Throwers looking for the best areas to throw to and varying their throws.

How Can I Change This?

- Use a lighter, slightly larger foam ball.
- Set up a smaller area.
- Allow catches on two bounces.
- Use a lower net and a larger, especially wider, area. This will encourage lower passes, almost like a volleyball dink pass. A higher net will make throwing and catching more difficult.

- Score points only when a ball is thrown out of bounds or when a partner fails to catch the ball on one bounce. This more traditional scoring rewards points for errors. The disadvantage of this scoring system is that it occurs *during* play rather than when a mistake stops play, so it could be distracting at first.
- Eliminate the bounce catch; require catches of aerial or fly balls only.

OVER LONG AND SHORT*

Prerequisites

- Skill in stationary bumping and setting and moving to bump and set
- Ability to control force and height of forearm passes and sets

Objectives

As a result of participating in this learning experience, children will improve their ability to

- Bump and set for accuracy to others without the pressure of competition
- Assist a partner in sending the ball across the net

Suggested Grade Range

Intermediate (5-6)

Organization

Three children play on one half of a volleyball court (area is one half of the width and the full length of the court); 1 player faces a net or rope, and the 2 other players are on the opposite side of the net (see Figure 8.3).

Equipment Needed

1 volleyball (or trainer volleyball) for each group of 3 children

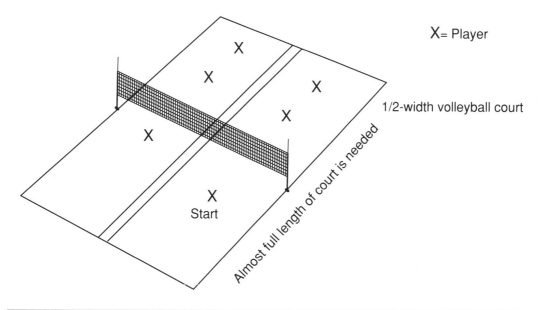

Figure 8.3   Over Long and Short.

*Note. From *Teaching Games in Physical Education* (staff development video) by the South Carolina Department of Education, 1984, Columbia, SC: South Carolina Department of Education. Copyright 1984 by the South Carolina Department of Education. Adapted by permission.

Description

"You have been doing very well in moving to bump and set. Today we are striving for accuracy when we do this. The 2 players on this side of the net try to place the ball back over the net so that it is easy for the 1 person on the other side of the net to play. That 1 person then plays a ball over the net that is easy for the front person to return, then next time plays the ball to the back person, then to the front person, and so on. See how Janna, Christopher, and Rae do this? [Students demonstrate.] We're trying to see how many passes we can make back and forth in a row. Start with an easy toss or self-set over the net. If a ball is *not* easy to play, a partner may play the ball to the other person on the same side; they may even use three hits to gain control and keep the accuracy game going. Make sure all of you get an equal chance at playing with a partner and playing one side by yourself. Try to play in your own area so that you don't interrupt other groups' activities. When I say 'Now,' get into groups of 3, get a ball that matches your skill level, set up, and begin. Now!

[After some play.] "Stop. See how this group is sending balls with enough height and a high arc, to allow teammates to move and align as well as they can? This controlled sending with enough height allows the partners to have time to send back a controlled pass. It works even when a partner has to move to align for the pass. Practice on this now. Go.

[Give feedback during play.] "Partners on one side, talk to each other, especially for balls in the area between you. When you feel as though you have enough skill, try counting how many passes you can make in a row. Try to improve on your best number as you practice. You will really have to concentrate.

[After more play.] "You did a good job of keeping the ball going back and forth. Next time, we will make this game harder by having you pass it to where your partner isn't. Be ready—it will be fun!" (See "How Can I Change This?")

Look For

- Players moving to align for the most optimal bumping or setting angle for returns.

- Partners communicating on balls that are between the back and front players.

How Can I Change This?

- Lower the net height.

- Allow one bounce prior to playing the highly arced balls.

- Practice the task but eliminate the net, moving the players closer if accuracy and force are too difficult.

- Return to partner practice on bumping and setting, including tries beginning from a self-set or easy throw.

- Have sets of partners on both sides of the net.

- Make the area slightly wider (12 to 15 feet on each side), and have players send balls to areas that defenders cannot guard well.

- Some groups may devise a scoring system. If you want to include a scoring system, it may be sufficient to give a point to a team when the other team fails to return the ball over the net or hits the ball out-of-bounds, or try a scoring system consistent with regulation volleyball rules.

- Try 3 players on each side.

TEACHABLE MOMENT

When a front player has to pass to a partner, what problem does this present for that player if he or she is a front player? It is difficult, especially because it may be unexpected, to position and align. The front person sometimes may have to turn away from the net to see and play the ball and then align to face the net and send it over the net. Propose this as a problem to solve. One easy solution is to play it back to the partner, who usually can position to face the net and, thus, play the ball over more easily. This also reinforces using the third hit, something that will be needed later when regulation volley- ball is played. Another solution would be to bump backward over one's head and across the net. This could lead to combination skill work and also relate to back setting. Another solution is the need to quickly move to align so that the ball can be received with vision and then sent over the net with vision. This means moving, turning, and turning quickly to align; this is a difficult skill and requires considerable practice.

THREE-COURT TENNIS

Prerequisites

- Racquet hitting with a partner, using both forehand and backhand strokes 5 to 10 times consecutively from 10 to 15 feet away
- Control bounce, an intermediate tap or hit to control the ball and to plan hitting action, using forehand and backhand strokes

Objectives

As a result of participating in this learning experience, children will improve their ability to

- Shift weight into the strike by stepping into the swing
- Adjust the ready position in relation to an approaching ball
- Control strokes to return balls with accuracy to two specified areas

Suggested Grade Range

Intermediate (5-6)

Organization

Two players are stationed in areas about 15 feet wide and 8 feet deep with a similar area between them.

Equipment Needed

1 light, short-handled racket per student; 1 tennis or foam ball for every 2 students; jump ropes to mark the middle area, and jump ropes, chalk, cones, or markers for the court boundaries for every 2 students

Description

"In this game, we'll be using 3 courts, but no net. We have 2 courts, just as in regular tennis, and we have 1 court, or box, in between the 2 end boxes. See them? Let's have Brittany and Terry go over and each stand in an end box. Yes, Terry, the box you are in belongs to you. Neither Brittany or Terry is allowed to move into the middle box.

"Now the object in this game is to return the ball to your partner before it bounces twice in your box. But, the ball must always bounce in the middle box once on the way to your partner. Let's watch these students to see how it goes; they have practiced before class because it's a little tricky at first. See how Brittany begins play by dropping the ball and hitting it with easy to medium force. The ball hits the middle area and bounces in Terry's box. Terry returns the ball to the middle area and then it bounces in Brittany's area. Great job! Play continues just like that.

"Let's review how we hit forehands and backhands. Somebody tell me something we've been stressing about these strokes. Yes, Jerry, step as we swing. Good, Ariel, keeping the racket level as we swing is important. Oh yes, Jonathan, keeping your side to the target or net—in this case the middle box—is something we need to remember. There is also one major difference. In regular tennis strokes, we worked on paddle to target, or continuing our swing. That worked well in longer distances. This game requires a lot of control because of that third area in the center. [Brittany and Terry keep hitting.] Notice how they have to use medium or light force to lift the ball so that it bounces in the middle box and rebounds, landing somewhere in the partner's box? This requires control rather than a lot of force. Questions? Yes, Alicia—if it bounces twice in your box before you hit it back, you and your partner decide what you want to happen. Yes, the other person could score a point. Or you could just start over and see how many hits you and your partner can get in a row. It's up to each set of partners. When I say 'Go,' get a partner, rackets, 1 ball, and markers, and begin. Go!

[During practice] "Now you are getting the idea of using light force and slightly lifting the ball. This is necessary to send the ball into the 2 target areas on the floor.

[During practice] "Amanda just asked if we can use control bounces. Who remembers what those are? Yes, Eddie, that's right. It's when you let the ball softly hit the face of the racket, bounce up, then bounce on the floor. Why do we do this? Yes, to control the ball better—so we have more time to decide where we want to hit it, to set up and control the hit, or both. Let's see if Anna can hit a ball to me, and I'll try to use a control bounce so you remember what it looks like. [Demonstrate.] You can use up to 3 control bounces if you choose to. No, the control bounces don't have to count as one of the 2 official bounces you're allowed to have. They're extra!

[During play] "I see many of you with your side to the other box. This helps you set up and step into the swing. Gabriele—nice stepping into the swing and using a controlled hit. Brandy is doing a good job of easily lifting the ball and placing it in the target areas. There are really two target areas, aren't there? Remember, after each hit, return to the best position to be able to cover the entire area.

[After some more practice] "Now, try to control the hits. Send the ball so that your partner has to move to set up and return it. If you're cooperating to see how many hits you can do in a row, try to hit the ball so your partner only has to move a little. If you are trying to make your partner miss, send the ball so that your partner has difficulty moving to the ball and little time to set up and hit. Some of you are playing cooperatively, and some are playing a competitive game where your partner is an opponent. Both kinds are good partner activities."

Look For

- Students moving to set up and step into the swing.
- Players using controlled hits and arcs to permit the ball to hit both target areas.
- Aiming to make the other player reposition.
- Positioning in relation to the ball for best coverage.

How Can I Change This?

- Use a larger rubber or foam ball for easier control; shorten the width of the middle area or allow players to use their hands as in foursquare.
- Eliminate the use of the control bounce.
- Widen the court area to increase movement and coverage, which increases difficulty.
- Add playing the ball on the volley.
- Substitute a net for the middle area. Encourage taking volleys when possible.

TEACHABLE MOMENT

Discuss different ways the ball can be hit with the racket. A level swing with the racket face moving like a door, perpendicular to the floor, is a basic stroke. Other methods include tilting the racket face upward or downward, depending on the height of contact; upward for low hits and higher or longer arcs; downward for high hits. The tilt of the racket can affect how the ball is sent. An upward tilt is called *open face*, while a downward tilt is called *closed face*.

Chapter 9

Learning Experiences for Invasion Games

Invasion games, including simple keep-away games, are popular with children. Some invasion games have overlap with tag, target, and fielding games. Invasion games focus on controlling and moving an object through another team's space or defending one's own space or goal area from the other team's advances. There are many variations. With some modifications, many invasion games can be changed from kicking to batting games, from throwing and catching to kicking games, and so on. One instructional goal is to have strategy concepts learned in one game transfer to similar invasion games.

It is difficult to predict exactly what a group of children will do, or fail to do, when playing a particular game or working on a specific game strategy. Teachers need to observe carefully and decide which strategies can be reinforced, which ones need to be emphasized, or whether the children can figure these out on their own during game play. Seven learning experiences provide a variety of ideas for invasion games.

Focus	Name	Suggested grade range
Defending a goal; creating and denying space when throwing	Hoop Guard	3-6
Defending a goal; creating and denying space when throwing and catching	Long Toss-n-Guard	3-6
Creating and denying space when throwing and catching	Trio Keep-Away	3-6
Creating and denying space when kicking	Triangle Soccer	4-6
Creating and denying space when throwing and catching	The Route of It All	5-6
Creating and denying space with kicking	Advance and Score Soccer	5-6
Creating and denying space with combination skills	Advance and Score Basketball	5-6

HOOP GUARD*

Prerequisites

- Proficiency in catching and throwing to oneself, to a partner, and to targets
- Ability to demonstrate a low body stance that is balanced (knees bent, feet apart and slightly staggered) and to quickly change one's body shape while keeping balanced
- Ability to move the arms and hands to block or strike an incoming object

Objectives

As a result of participating in this learning experience, children will improve their ability to

- Fake and then quick-release to aim at a target guarded by another person
- Use one's hands, body parts, and body to catch, block, or reduce the chances of a throw getting past to the target goal
- Create space to position better for a throw (3-4, #20)

Suggested Grade Range

Intermediate (3-6)

Organization

This game is played in pairs in an area 20 feet by 10 feet. One child has a beanbag and stands within 15 feet of, but not closer than 3 to 5 feet in front of, a hoop lying on the ground. The other child stands behind, inside, or in front of the hoop. The playing area has 5 feet behind the hoop and is about 10 feet wide (see Figure 9.1).

Equipment Needed

1 beanbag (or small foam ball) and 1 hoop for each pair of students; existing lines on the floor (or tape, chalk, or water-soluble shoe polish)

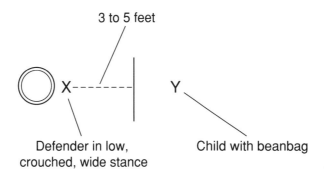

Figure 9.1 Hoop Guard.

*Note. From "A Dynamic Approach to Teaching Games in Elementary PE" by S. Doolittle and K.T. Girard, 1991, *Journal of Physical Education, Recreation and Dance*, **62**(4), pp. 57-62. Copyright 1991 by the American Alliance for Health, Physical Education, Recreation and Dance. Adapted by permission.

Description

"Today we're going to play a game I think you'll like! It's called Hoop Guard. See how it's set up? A person with a beanbag—the thrower—is about 10 feet away from a partner, who is defending or guarding a hoop. If you are the thrower, you may move anywhere except past the line that is in front of the defender's hoop. You try to place or throw the beanbag inside the hoop. You may run with the beanbag, fake throws, and change direction before attempting a throw, but you cannot slide the beanbag hard along the floor to hit the hoop. Respect your partner; do not throw the beanbag hard right at your partner.

"The defender also should use good balance, fakes, changes of position, and movement to keep the thrower from getting a good try at the hoop goal. The defender may use any part of the body to block the beanbag.

"If a goal is scored or missed, either player may get the beanbag and continue the game. Remember, this is a fast game. There is no bumping or pushing. When I say 'Go,' get a partner, a hoop, and a beanbag or a small sponge ball; then set up and begin. [Pause.] Go.

[After some play.] "Stop. Where is a good position to stand when your partner has the beanbag? [Near the hoop, between the partner and the hoop.] Does this depend on how far from your hoop the opponent is? [You need not be as close nor as ready if the thrower is far away.] How can you position yourself or stand so that you are most ready to intercept or block the beanbag and keep it from going into your hoop area? [Low, wide body stance with hands moving to fake and ready for quick movement in any direction; eyes on the beanbag and thrower's movements.] Let's think of these as we begin again. Go."

Look For

- Positioning so that the guard may move quickly in any direction.

- Faking to draw a particular kind of throw or to distract the thrower.

- Thrower using fakes and changes of directions to freeze the guard or get space for a shot attempt.

How Can I Change This?

- Use a softer object that does not bounce.

- Increase the size of the target to make offense easier.

- Move the hoop closer to the restraining line if the offense needs help or farther away if the defense needs help.

- Stop play after a shot attempt, set again, and begin the game. Each person gets 2 to 4 tries, and then players exchange roles.

- Reduce the size of the target (place a detergent bottle inside the hoop as the goal) to make offense harder.

- With jump ropes (or elastic ropes, chalk, or other markings), make a circle 3 to 5 feet outside the hoop. The thrower moves around the outside of the larger circle, changing directions quickly and faking to attempt a shot inside the hoop at the target bottle. The defender must guard the entire hoop by moving sideways around the hoop.

- An extension of the variation just described involves 3 players—1 defender and 2 offensive players (see Figure 9.2). The defender protects the goal by sliding around the outside of the goal hoop or even moving over the hoop. The other 2 players may pass the beanbag and try for goals, making the defender's job more difficult.

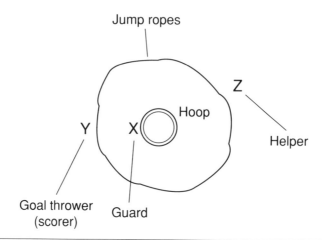

Figure 9.2   2-on-1 variation of Hoop Guard.

TEACHABLE MOMENTS

Discuss a situation where one partner is almost always successful and the other is not successful very often—how would each of them feel? What changes could be made to make the game more even? [Increase the restraining line distance or reduce the target area for the more successful player.]

If a defender comes out to guard the thrower to prevent that person from getting close to the target, what problems does that present to the thrower? [The defender's movement and body positioning can impede the thrower's movement closer to the target and throwing angles and space.] What advantages? [If the thrower can get past the defender, an open shot on goal is possible; if time permits, the open goal invites a long goal attempt.]

LONG TOSS-N-GUARD*

Prerequisites

- Ability to move with an object and throw with some accuracy at a stationary target
- Ability to use one's body to block or deflect a thrown object
- Success in playing Hoop Guard
- Ability to get open for a pass
- Ability to time passes so that partner can reach to catch

Objectives

As a result of participating in this learning experience, children will improve their ability to

- Use fakes and variety in quick-release throws to aim at a target guarded by another person
- Use hands, body parts, and body to catch, block, or reduce the chances of a throw getting past them to the target goal
- Make the transition quickly from offense to defense after a score or shot attempt (3-4, #20)
- Position to catch and throw with a partner

Suggested Grade Range

Intermediate (3-6)

Organization

Each of two partners has a hoop positioned about 30 feet apart. Each player can move anywhere in the 40 feet by 10 feet playing space except the last 8 to 10 feet near the opponent's hoop when a player is trying to score. There is a restraining line 3 to 5 feet in front of the opponent's hoop and another 5 feet behind each hoop (see Figure 9.3).

Equipment Needed

1 beanbag (or small foam ball) and 2 hoops for each pair of students; existing lines on the floor (or tape, chalk, or water-soluble shoe polish)

Description

"Remember our Hoop Guard game? This is like it, but a little harder. Laura and Sherry will demonstrate it. [Explain while students demonstrate.] Two hoops are on the floor about this far apart [20 to 35 feet]. The person with the beanbag, in this case, Laura, tries to throw the beanbag so that it goes inside Sherry's hoop. Laura can move anywhere except past the line about 5 feet in front of Sherry's hoop in order to throw the beanbag.

"Laura's job, after she throws the beanbag, is to then keep Sherry from throwing the beanbag into *her* hoop. Sliding the beanbag hard along the floor to hit the hoop or hit and move inside the hoop doesn't count. Respect your partner; try not to throw the beanbag hard right at your partner. If you prefer, use a small sponge ball. Remember, after a score or a miss, play continues. So be aware that you will have to retrieve the object and try to shoot again, or quickly change to become a good defender. When I say 'Go,' groups of 2 will need to get 2 hoops, and 1 beanbag or small sponge ball; then set up and begin. [Pause.] Go.

*Note. From "A Dynamic Approach to Teaching Games in Elementary PE" by S. Doolittle and K.T. Girard, 1991, *Journal of Physical Education, Recreation and Dance*, **62**(4), pp. 57-62. Copyright 1991 by the American Alliance for Health, Physical Education, Recreation and Dance. Adapted by permission.

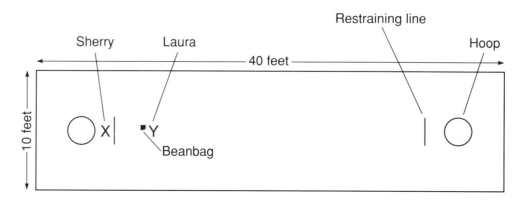

Figure 9.3   Long Toss-n-Guard.

[After some practice.] "OK, everyone stop and come in close to me. Where is a good position to stand when your opponent has the beanbag? Does this depend on how far from your hoop the opponent is? [1 to 3 feet in front of the goal you're defending when your opponent is approaching the hoop; very close in balanced, ready position if the thrower is very close. You may go out toward your opponent to keep him or her from getting close, but be ready to move back to defend the goal if this doesn't work well.] How can you position yourself or stand so that you are most ready to intercept or block the beanbag and keep it from going into your hoop area? Is there anything you used in Hoop Guard that can be helpful in today's game? [As in Hoop Guard, a low, wide body stance with hands moving to fake but ready to permit quick movement in any direction; eyes on the beanbag and thrower's movements.] Good. Let's practice again, focusing on being a good defender. Go.

[After some play.] "Stop. What problems do you have as the thrower when you're very close to your opponent's hoop? [You could miss the shot, and then you're a long distance from the hoop you must defend. You must be ready to guard closely to prevent the opponent from advancing or making a shot attempt, or quickly move back to guard the hoop. This is called a transition from offense to defense.] Is it better to make a short toss or a long toss at the hoop? Why? [It depends. A short toss may have more chance of scoring but will probably be defended better. A long toss may be easier to do because the defender isn't as close to or as ready for this kind of shot.] OK, this time let's have the throwers focus on where they are when they throw, and the kinds of throws they use. Go.

[At lesson closure.] "What strategies did you try that worked?"

Look For

- Quick transitions back to guard the hoop after a player throws at the opponent's hoop. (Some children will be so interested in seeing the results of their own throws that they will forget to move back to play defense. It is less likely, but also possible, that a child will hurry throws or even throw without aiming or using any strategy.)

- Students' original ideas and reasons for various ways of throwing and defending (ask students to explain these).

How Can I Change This?

- Increase the size of the target to make offense easier. Add 1 or more hoops for each player to guard.

- Make the players more restricted in how close they can get to the partner's hoop; for example, put a line about halfway between the hoops.

- Reduce the size of the target (put a detergent bottle inside the hoop) to make offense harder.
- Remove the 5-foot zone restriction to make defense harder.
- Make it a game for 4 players, 2 teams of 2. Each team has 1 player positioned on each side of the playing space. There is a center dividing line that no one may cross. Offensive players may pass to teammates; defenders try to intercept a pass or keep opponent from receiving a pass, or defenders move to guard the hoop goal.
- Make it a 6-person game; 1 player on each team may cross the center line and play both offense and defense. This is similar to the roving player that was used in women's 6-person basketball (see Figure 9.4).

TEACHABLE MOMENT

If one partner is almost always successful and the other is not successful very often, how would each one feel? What changes could be made to make the game more even? [Increase the restraining line distance or reduce the target area for the more successful player.]

Beanbag

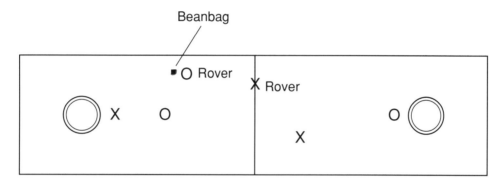

Figure 9.4   Team Toss-n-Guard.

TRIO KEEP-AWAY

Prerequisites

- Ability to throw balls to a partner while stationary or moving at slow to medium speeds
- Ability to move to catch balls thrown by a partner
- Practice moving to get to a safe and advantageous space after passing the ball

Objectives

As a result of participating in this learning experience, students will improve their ability to

- Time passes to avoid being tagged by the defender (5-6, #7)
- Adjust the throw based on position and shape of defender
- Move without the ball to reposition for a catch
- Use a variety of jumps, reaches, body shapes, and quick body movements to tag the person with ball, cause an errant throw, or deflect or intercept a pass

Suggested Grade Range

Intermediate (3-6)

Organization

Groups of 3 players (2 on offense and 1 on defense) move within a 12- to 15-foot square space.

Equipment Needed

1 ball (#4 foam ball or 7- to 8-inch diameter rubber ball) for each group; 4 cones (or other boundary markers) per group

Description

"Our game today is going to be fun and challenging. It's played in groups of 3. Two partners position themselves anywhere within the area marked off by the 4 cones [approximately 12 to 15 foot square]. The third player is the defender and is also allowed to be anywhere in the playing area. The object for the partners, the offense, is to pass the ball eight times without having the defender catch the ball, or tag you while you are holding the ball, or having the ball go out-of-bounds. If eight passes are caught successfully, set up again with a new defender. Take turns being the defender. To be good at this game, partners, you will need to pass the ball after you get the defender to come close to you, but not close enough to tag you. Try to think of ways to pass the ball so that the defender cannot tag you or intercept the ball. Defenders, you need to decide whom to tag, or how to intercept. Anytime you need to, the partners can take a short time-out to discuss what they're doing and what they need to do. When I say 'Go,' get in a group of 3, decide who is what, set up your playing area away from other groups, and begin the game. Go!

[Allow several minutes of playing time so that you can observe the behaviors listed in the "Look For" section.]

"Stop. Let's watch this group here as they play for a while. When is Jennifer passing the ball? Where is the defender when Jennifer passes the ball? [Jennifer passes when the defender is coming close to her but not close enough to tag her.] How do Jennifer and Cody get the defender, Marcia, to come toward them? [They wait if Marcia (the defender) is far away. They use fake passes to make her change what she is doing.]

"This is a harder question. When a partner fakes a high pass, what does the defender tend to do? [The defender moves high for a high pass fake.] Now, what type of pass would work best if you faked a high pass and the defender jumped high to try to intercept? That's right, a low pass, even a bounce pass. How about if you faked a low pass and the defender moved low with outstretched arms to the side? Good idea, use a higher pass. Let's go back and try to work on waiting for defenders to come toward you, faking, and using passes that will cause the most difficulty for the defender. Go.

[After a longer period of play.] "Stop. So far, we have been working to help the people with the ball. If you are the defender, what can you do to be more successful? [Don't let the partners know when you will be changing body positions or moving quickly; fake one thing and do another; move slowly toward a partner and then speed up to confuse the passer; change what you are doing so that the partners can't always tell or predict what you will do.] When we begin again, defenders work hard on one new idea that you haven't used before, or try each of these to find out what works for you. Who can prevent eight passes for the next [give time limit]? Go.

[After a period of play.] "Stop. I also noticed only in the last minute or so that some of you are passing and then moving to another area. At first, that confused your partner, but your partner saw you do that and then adjusted. Now that movement presents problems for the defender, who cannot see you well without turning his or her head. That has some real advantages for those of you with the ball—the offense. Can you do this more often as you continue? I also noticed that defenders are using more fakes, too. Defenders are quickly changing what they do, and that is forcing the partners to think longer or be less sure what to do. Very much improved defense. Go.

[After a period of play.] "Stop. I'm beginning to see defenders thinking ahead and actually anticipating what the offense will do. Let's watch Dirk, Benjamin, and Caron as they play. Caron is defending. Can you explain what Caron is doing that helps you figure out what the passing team is likely to do? [Moving to where the pass is expected; changing defensive position; jumping or moving unexpectedly just as the pass is made; showing one position (low and wide) and then changing it quickly; looking at the person with the ball but also trying to think where the other person will be.] As we begin again, let's try several of these ideas to help make you a better defender. Go."

Look For

- Offensive players making passes into the defender's weakness (e.g., low or bounce passes when the defender is stretched high or jumping).
- Offensive players using fakes or timing passes well (not too soon or very late).
- Offensive players moving, if to their advantage, after they pass the ball.
- Defenders concealing their intended movements, including using fakes.
- Defensive play, not just offensive play, so that strategies are reinforced through play (S. Doolittle, personal communication, July 10, 1992).

How Can I Change This?

- Have the defender show a weak and telegraphed movement so that the offense has more time to decide when to pass and fewer decisions to make.
- Add a 5-second rule for passing—the ball must be passed within 5 seconds (or another fair time limit).
- Decrease the playing area.
- Require that the receiver move prior to receiving a pass.
- Require that the receiver be moving when receiving a pass.

- Change the object caught to a more difficult shape, or reduce the ball size.
- Require that the passer be in the air when the pass is made.

TEACHABLE MOMENTS

Partners need to expect some poor passes and encourage and help their teammates instead of criticizing or blaming them. Good players applaud a good performance, even if it is on the other team.

If a defender stays with the partner who does *not* have the ball, this presents serious problems for the passer. It even destroys the game, because nothing can happen. Actually, the defender has won the game. The only way the game can continue is if the receiving partner moves to get away from the defender. This strategy is an important one that you can emphasize when it is observed.

TRIANGLE SOCCER

Prerequisites

- Success with Trio Keep-Away
- Skill in trapping kicked balls coming from a variety of angles and then passing accurately to a partner who is stationary or moving
- Ability to monitor where 2 teammates are while trapping and passing a ball quickly and accurately
- Ability to defend more than 1 player
- Skill in positioning to use or guard the available space

Objectives

As a result of participating in this learning experience, children will improve their ability to

- Keep the offensive setup in a triangle to allow passes in either direction (5-6, #5)
- Position and defend to make passes difficult and to intercept passes (5-6, #8)
- Create and use passing lanes

Suggested Grade Range

Intermediate (4-6)

Organization

Three players form a triangle (actually positioned at three corners of an incomplete square); they stand 20 to 35 feet apart. A 4th player, the defender, is in the center of the other 3 (see Figure 9.5).

Equipment Needed

1 ball (#4 or #5 foam ball or soccer ball) for each group of 4 players

Description

"Remember Trio Keep-Away, which we played some time ago? Sort of? Today we will play a game like that, but we'll be limited to trapping and passing *without* using our hands and arms. Let's look at the group here. Megan, Roberto, and Alicia are positioned

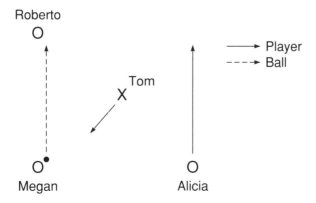

Figure 9.5   Triangle Soccer.

in a triangle. If Megan at the point of the triangle passes to Roberto on the left and Roberto moves a little to get the ball, then Alicia must move, too, so that Roberto has a player open for a pass. Let's watch them for several passes to see how this works. [Class observes four to five passes.] It is important that you always keep this triangle. Can we do that? When I say 'Now,' get in groups of 4. Each group needs one ball and a space of its own. One person—the helper—will organize the other 3 into a triangle. When the group is ready, raise your hands and watch me. You have 15 seconds to get organized. Now.

[After 15 seconds.] "Good, that was very quick. The helper needs to observe the group carefully so that the group always keeps in the triangle position. Try five passes. Helpers, give the others suggestions about how to keep the triangle and how to move after they pass. After five passes, have another person be the helper. Go.

[After some time to practice.] "Stop. This time, the helper can stand in the middle to watch closer and to be an obstacle the others must pass around. If you hit the person in the middle, you are not passing to the left or right on the outside of the triangle. Understand? Keep playing. Try to see if you can make five good passes in a row and still keep the triangle. Stop and change people after five good passes are made in a row. Go.

[After considerable time at this application task.] "Stop. Now let's see what happens when Tom, in the middle, becomes a defender. The idea is to pass the ball so that Tom cannot get it. Do you remember what strategies the offense used in Trio Keep-Away? What were some of these? That's right—wait until the defender is coming close, but not too close. Good, Marcia—fake a pass to trick the defender. Yes, Roberto. Be sure to move to help your partner out. Let's try these strategies. Change the person in the middle when a ball is intercepted or after five successful passes. Begin.

[During, but after some, practice.] "If the ball gets outside and away from the playing area, the nearest player must retrieve it while the teammates move to try to maintain the triangle setup. [After repeated practice.] Stop. What do you think is the best time to pass? That's right—when the defender is far away from a passing lane. A passing lane should be open—no one should be in it—when passes are made. A *passing lane* actually means creating space so an easy pass can be made. To create space, you have to look at where your teammates are before you pass, and they should look at you and the defender to see how they can help you make a safe passing lane. Let's see if you can do this. Make sure to pass only when your lane is open. Go.

[At lesson closure.] "We'll also practice more of this later, because creating space for safe passes is very important in many games."

Look For

- Offensive players looking at the defender and teammates before deciding what to do.
- Good trapping and accurate passing (not just hard, inaccurate kicking).
- Variation in the defender's faking, positioning, and movement strategy.
- The opposite partners on offense moving to keep the triangle.
- Faking, including body turning, by offensive players to confuse the defender.
- Fakes with either foot by the offense, stepping over the ball and passing in the opposite direction, and using other fakes and kicks practiced earlier with a partner.
- Passing lanes remaining open.

How Can I Change This?

- Move back to partner work that emphasizes smooth trapping and quick passing to a stationary or a moving partner, if needed.
- Allow no more than three touches for each pass.

- Require the player with the ball to move the ball before passing; do not allow the ball to be stationary.
- Place a time limit on the passing.
- Reduce the size of the playing area to make offense more difficult.
- Put a second defensive player in the center as an obstacle; this player may not intercept the ball and must stand still in the center of the triangle.
- If playing room permits, reset the triangle even when a pass goes outside the area.
- Change to 5 players passing left, right, and across a circle to avoid 2 defenders.
- Modify game to use striking, catching, or throwing skills.

TEACHABLE MOMENT

What kind of vision helps a person with the ball, or even a defender, look at his or her teammates, without having to look directly at them? Discuss peripheral or side vision and how it can help offensive and defensive players.

THE ROUTE OF IT ALL

Prerequisites

- Skill in both throwing and catching while moving and changing patterns
- Ability to shadow another player closely without interfering with that person's running directions
- Experience in moving backward quickly and in turning the body while keeping balanced; skill in the grapevine dance step and its variations
- Experience receiving a thrown ball or a centered ball and then passing accurately to a moving person

Objectives

As a result of participating in this learning experience, children will improve their ability to

- Run prescribed patterns with faking, speed, and direction changes in order to catch a thrown ball
- Pass to a guarded teammate (5-6, #7)
- Guard a player and try to intercept a pass, deflect the ball, or keep the other player from catching the ball (5-6, #8)

Suggested Grade Range

Intermediate (5-6)

Organization

Groups of 2, then 3, in outdoor space that is 10×20 yards or larger

Equipment Needed

1 large poster showing Figure 9.6; per group: 1 junior-size or smaller foam football (or a 5-inch rubber ball), 1 clipboard holding 1 laminated pass routes card (see Figure

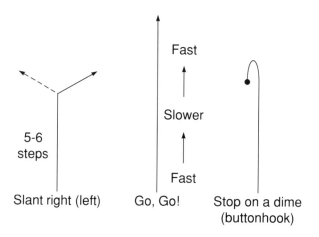

Figure 9.6   The Route of It All.

9.6) and 1 figure of defensive footwork (Figure 9.7), and 6 orange cones (or other boundary markers)

Description

"You have practiced throwing passes to partners who were running many kinds of pathways, just as they do in football. It's challenging to throw both long and short passes to a partner. And receivers must learn to catch these while running at or near full speed. But receivers also need to be able to quickly change direction and then catch. Look at this chart. [Point to poster-size version of Figure 9.6.] Today we'll practice using these pass-catching pathways. We'll call them *pass routes*. But first, when I say 'Go,' find a partner and select a ball of your choice. Then begin practicing short, easy catches while the receiver is moving at a slow or medium speed. Does anyone remember where the passer wants to aim the ball so the receiver can catch it? Good, Juan, chest level. Receivers, make sure you start on one side of the passer and then move across in front of them at a slant so that you move away from, rather than closer to, the passer as you run.

[During practice.] "Receivers, you will need to move four to five steps and then change direction by slanting right or left, looking back for the ball. Passers, be sure to throw so that your receiver has to reach to catch. To do this, the ball needs to be thrown ahead of where they are going, even though they are moving at a slow or medium speed. Think about this, and see how many you can complete in a row.

[After further practice.] "Stop and come in to me quickly. Partners, get a clipboard and look at the pass routes. This time, receivers will begin by standing beside the passer. On a signal, the receiver will run directly away from the passer and run one of the pass routes drawn on the laminated cards: the slant right, the slant left, or the Go, Go! For the Go, Go!, you can slow down and then suddenly sprint very fast, or you can fake a slant and then go quickly straight down the field. Partners, tell each other the pass ahead of time so that you both know what is going to happen. Throwers may wait and may pretend to receive a pass from center and drop back several steps while

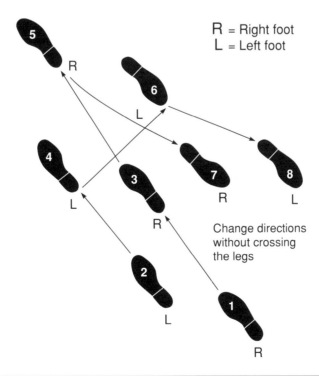

Figure 9.7 Defensive footwork.

watching the receiver run. Change roles after running one or two routes. Keep score of how many good passes and receptions you and your partner complete out of each 10 tries.

[During subsequent practice.] "Make sure that you make very clear and distinct changes in the angles you move in. I see faking one way, then abruptly going in the other direction. That will make it difficult for a defender to know what you're going to do. On long routes, you could start slowly and then go really fast, pretending that a defender was trying to keep near you. [After subsequent practice.] On the next route, run very fast as though as you were going very deep, then quickly slow down, turn around, and stop to face the thrower. This is a buttonhook pattern. Throwers, you must time your pass so that the receiver can catch it soon after turning and stopping. Otherwise, a defender could recover and get close or even intercept the pass. Here is a laminated card for the buttonhook pattern.

[After additional practice, or begin here, if appropriate.] "You already know how to run the pass patterns on the laminated cards. This time we'll work in groups of 3. One player will be on defense and will try to shadow the receiver as that player moves to catch the ball. The receiver and the passer talk, so both know what they will be doing. The defender doesn't know, and that makes it challenging. Let's watch Ellis and Jill and Alva a couple of times. [After watching.] The passer, Jill, tries to send the ball so that it arrives as the catcher, Alva, speeds up or changes the running pattern. That is hard to do, but Jill was able to time her passes very well. *Timing* is important for the passer. The catcher needs to make sharp changes. And the defender needs to shadow closely and try to anticipate when the ball is coming. When I say 'Begin,' get into groups of 3 and go to one of the areas marked by 6 orange cones. At each game area, there is a clipboard with choices of running routes. Here is a picture of the routes. [Hold up diagram shown in Figure 9.6.] Also on the clipboard is a picture of defensive footwork. Defenders will need to turn their bodies when needed but should try to *not* cross their feet. Like this. [Demonstrate the footwork shown in Figure 9.7.] You have practiced the footwork before. After three passing attempts, change roles so that everyone gets practice at all roles. Begin.

[After some practice.] "Make your direction changes very quickly, and use fakes just before you make the *cut* or change. Remember to vary your speed. The secret is to make the change quickly but not always to run fast. Defenders, react to what you *expect* the receiver to do and also to what the receiver *does*. Try not to react to fakes, but to what actually is the real change.

"Defenders, you need to vary what you are doing by sometimes beginning further away and sometimes closer to the receiver. You can run backward, but you should use the grapevine footwork if at all possible. Try to deflect the pass or even catch it when you can."

Look For

- Clear running routes with fakes and quick changes in direction or speed.
- Passers timing passes well.
- Defenders making smooth and quick reactions to catchers' route changes.

How Can I Change This?

- To make this easier for the defense, put a time restriction of 5 seconds on the offense, reduce the space, first in length, then in width, or, before play begins, show the defense two (or three) routes—one of which will be used for that play.
- To make this easier for the offense, use a 5-inch ball or a foam football or tell the defender to play deeper or closer to the starting line when play begins.
- To make this harder for the defense, allow time for the catcher to make two or more route changes or encourage planning of other routes. (Be aware that this conference time could take much of the available time for one lesson.)

- To make this harder for the offense, add a beginning throw from a center who then rushes the passer, perhaps after a count to five. Pressure the passer, tag the passer, or try to jump or deflect the pass.
- Try 2-on-2, with each team allowed four chances to move the ball forward a designated distance that the group determines is challenging for both the offense and defense.
- Practice with 2 receivers, with or without defenders.

TEACHABLE MOMENT

Communication between the thrower and catcher is very important. Discuss what types of communication are helpful and nonhelpful.

ADVANCE AND SCORE SOCCER

Prerequisites

- Ability to change direction quickly while running and foot-dribbling, varying direction, force, and speed
- Ability to shadow a partner who dribbles
- Ability to dribble, pass, and receive ground, bouncing, and aerial balls with 1 or 2 partners while all are moving
- Ability to dribble and avoid losing the ball when guarded by 1 defender who plays active defense
- Success in simple 2-on-1 and 3-on-1 keep-away

Objectives

As a result of participating in this learning experience, students will improve their ability to

- Create space by moving without the ball to receive a pass, or by forcing the defender to guard 1 player so that the partner can move to a more advantageous position (5-6, #8)
- Use wait time and fakes to lure defender closer and then pass successfully (5-6, #8)
- Position themselves defensively to make forward progress and passes difficult, using fakes and moving to deny space or cut off passes (5-6, #8)

Suggested Grade Range

Intermediate (5-6)

Organization

Groups of 4 play in a 30-foot square (or slightly larger) area; 2 offensive players move toward a goal against 1 defender; the other player is a temporary coach while waiting for a turn to play.

Equipment Needed

1 #4 foam soccer ball (or partially deflated 7- or 8-inch rubber ball) per group of 4; 2 cones

Description

"Today we'll play minisoccer, complete with your own coach. We'll work in groups of 4—2 offensive players, 1 defender, and 1 coach, who gives helpful feedback to both sides. The offensive players begin about 30 feet from two cones which are the goal. Their task is to send the ball between the cones. The defender will try to keep them from scoring. Just to review, what happens when a defender goes way out to guard the player with the ball? [The defender must guard both opponents and also guard the goal; going way out gives the offense too much advantage.] What happens if the defender closely guards the player who does not have the ball? [The player with the ball dribbles in and shoots.] When I say 'Go,' get into groups of 4, set the playing area, and begin. After three attempts (successful or unsuccessful) to advance on the goal, remember to rotate roles so that everyone gets the same number of attempts at offense, defense, and coaching. Offense, remember to time your passes carefully. Go.

[After some play or while players are setting up.] "Defenders, remember to conceal what you're going to do. Change speed and body positions to make passing and shooting more difficult for the offense. Getting too close to or too far away from the player with the ball would give the offense an advantage. It makes it easier for them to pass and score. Of course, the closer the defender is to the goal, the easier it is to guard both offensive players. They simply don't have much room to work in. But, the ball is also very close to the goal, so that becomes a danger, too. As a defender, you need to remember these options.

[Give specific reinforcement feedback.] "Nice, Mary, you passed just when the defender was getting close to you. That gives your partner time to get control and look to see where you will be. Remember, don't let the defender know too early what you'll do. That's called *telegraphing* the pass. Coaches, help both the offense and the defense. Position yourselves on the other side of the goal to retrieve shot attempts.

"The offensive players without the ball need to move so that the defenders do not know exactly where they are or where they'll be receiving the ball. The partner with the ball must use faking and looking around to confuse the defender. Keep the defender guessing.

"Oh, Ian just moved behind the defender across to the other side of the area. Allison, who had the ball, dribbled slightly to the side where the partner was to lure the defender that way. Just then, she passed to the other side, timing the ball perfectly. There was nothing the defender, Shawn, could do, even though playing very good defense. Good job, Ian and Allison.

[When observed, Ryan, a coach, explains what occurred in his group. He says,] "Taylor just made a good pass and then moved to reposition nicely. Good work. Defenders, you must change your position when the offense does. Try to block easy passes by not allowing a straight and easy pathway for a pass. Good, Arnold, you kept changing your defensive position and prevented an easy straight pass."

"Stop. Now we'll place the coach on the other side of the goal area away from the play. When a shot is attempted, the coach stops the ball, and the coach and his or her teammate, the active defender, move to offense. One of the previous offensive players becomes the defender; the other becomes the coach. The same 2 players always are a team. Change teams after 6 changes of possession of the ball. This means after 6 interceptions, missed shots, or goals. Adjust the playing area if you need more room.

[During play.] "Defenders are beginning to get in the way of passes. Good work. We'll call this *clogging the passway* [see Figure 9.8].

[After additional play or when groups are ready.] "Stop. You have practiced passing a ball to a partner and moving to receive a return pass. This is called a *give-and-go* pass. It's sort of like a rebounding wall pass. Pass to a partner and then move to receive

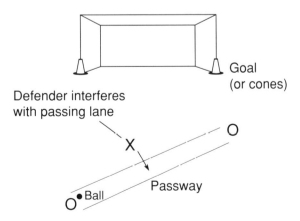

Figure 9.8   Look for the defense to clog the opponents' passways.

a return pass. See the poster I'm holding. [Hold up a poster with diagram like that shown in Figure 9.9.] Give-and-go passing is very effective in soccer and other team games.

"But if that's all you do, the defense will be able to predict pretty easily what you will do. So, another type of passing that is useful is called a *through* pass. Look at the poster. [Hold up poster with diagram like that shown in Figure 9.9.] If the defender thinks you are going to do a give-and-go pass, what will the defender do? [Go to that side to block the passway.] Instead of waiting to receive a pass, the player without the ball runs toward the goal, and then the person with the ball passes to him or her. The pass can actually go behind the defender while that defender is moving to block the give-and-go pass. For every strategy the defense uses, the offense holds another strategy. The offense needs both the give-and-go and the through pass. Let's try to use these passes as we continue play."

Look For

- Whether the coach knows what to look for and give feedback on. There may be a need to stop individual games and help the players, or children can have conference times, with or without the coach's help.
- Defense setting up to cut off easy passing pathways (passways) (see Figure 9.8).
- Offense using fakes and movement to create a better passing lane.
- Give-and-go and through passing (see Figure 9.9).

How Can I Change This?

- Have players advance to a goal line without taking a shot.
- Restrict the defense if the offense has little success by adding a third offensive player so that options increase.
- Limit the number of passes or time the offense has to get in position and take a shot. Limit the number of ball touches for a person's possession.
- Add a goalie so that the game becomes 2 against 1 defender and 1 goalie (if appropriate goalie instruction has occurred).
- Place the 4th student (the coach) in as a 2nd defender, at first just standing or walking, then playing normal defense.
- Extend to 3-on-2 soccer.
- This can easily be modified for a throwing-and-catching or striking-and-receiving game.

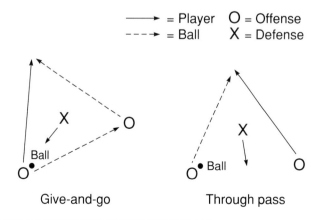

Figure 9.9   Look for basic passing strategies.

TEACHABLE MOMENT

Allow children to change rules to make the game more challenging and fun, especially if a defensive person is consistently beaten by a highly successful offense. Making passing difficult may be as important as intercepting the ball, because beginning players may not pass well. So the defender can choose *not* to try to intercept but to position to make passes difficult. An important concept, but a difficult one, is to realize that giving up some space toward the goal is not necessarily weak defense. As space becomes smaller, it is easier to defend because there are fewer passing lanes. Identify and discuss other important concepts.

ADVANCE AND SCORE BASKETBALL

Prerequisites

- Ability to change direction quickly while running and hand-dribbling, varying force and speed
- Ability to receive various kinds of passes while moving and to subsequently pass, dribble, and shoot at a goal
- Practice moving to get free from imaginary and actual defenders to receive a pass
- Ability to position well on defense and impede another's progress in dribbling and passing

Objectives

As a result of participating in this learning experience, students will improve their ability to

- Create space by moving without the ball to receive a pass, or by forcing the defender to guard 1 player so that the partner can move to a more advantageous position (5-6, #8)
- Wait and fake to lure the defender closer and then pass successfully and also to move toward the goal during wait time if the defender stays away (5-6, #8)
- Position themselves defensively to make forward progress and passes difficult, using fakes and moving to deny space or cut off passes (5-6, #8)

Suggested Grade Range

Intermediate (5-6)

Organization

Groups of 4 play in 30-foot square (or slightly smaller) area; 2 offensive players move toward a goal against 1 defender; the other player is a temporary coach.

Equipment Needed

1 rubber ball that bounces well and 1 basketball goal (or a large barrel or wall target); 1 pencil and some paper per group of 4

Description

"Today we have our own minibasketball game. Two players, Kyle and Kristin, stand apart and about 20 feet from the goal. They will pass and dribble the ball, move to create open areas for each other, and advance the ball closer to the goal so that one of them may take a shot that has a good chance of going in the basket. A defender, Richard, will try to keep this from happening. Let's see how this works as we watch them. [Kyle, Kristin, and Richard practice several times.] Notice how Kyle and Kristin use fakes to try to keep Richard guessing about what they will do. Oh, that was interesting! Richard stayed close to Kristin, so Kyle started to dribble directly to the basket. That forced Richard to come over. Just then Kyle passed to Kristin, who had moved a little closer to the basket. That kind of play sure puts a lot of pressure on the defender. I asked Richard to do this to help you see how this can work. But Richard will use all his defensive skills when he plays today.

"Elizabeth, we'll put you in as a coach. The coach gets to give advice to both the offense and defense. Coaches should look at what players are doing and tell them what they can do to be more successful. They might want to call a time-out, if needed. Change roles after each two or three tries so everyone gets about the same time in each role. At the end of 10 minutes, we'll ask each group to write down a list of strategies that were successful on defense and on offense. When I say 'Begin,' groups of 4 will need to get a ball and set up away from other groups. Each group needs a pencil and a piece of paper, too. Begin.

[See Advance and Score Soccer for expected performance and sample feedback comments. These ideas will not be repeated in this example. Be aware that students may tend to dribble first without looking for a pass or to dribble too long once a dribble is deemed advisable.]

[Give specific feedback.] "I like the way Juanita watched her teammate while she was dribbling. Juanita was able to look for her teammate and also occasionally look at the ball. She kept her head up and only looked at the ball with her outside, or peripheral, vision.

"The strategy sequence is, First look for a shot, then look to see if a teammate is open for a pass, then, and only then, dribble. Try to look for a shot, then pass to a teammate who is closer to the basket or unguarded *first*. You'll want to dribble last. This requires a lot of cooperation.

[Give more feedback.] "Miri, you took the shot. Good work. You were not guarded and were close enough for a good try.

"Travis, you began to dribble without looking for a shot or for your teammate. Try to use our strategy sequence. Shoot, pass, dribble. It will work.

"Good idea, Coach Nicole. You wanted the defense to keep changing the movements, timing of jumps, and fakes. It worked. The offense had more difficulty completing passes and was unable to get in a position for a good shot try."

[When passes are late, such as when a player gets open and then has to wait for a pass, the team loses quality. Players must be alert to teammates' movements so that passes are timed to take advantage of the moving that occurs.]

Look For

- Whether the coach knows what to look for and give feedback on.

- Offensive players changing their alignment so that the person who began on the left side moves to the right while the partner moves to the left side (It might be good to point this out to the entire class when it happens).

- Defenders who deny space by cutting off clear passing lanes.

How Can I Change This?

- Restrict the defense by having the defender play very high with many jumps if the offense relies too much on high passes and avoids bounce and low passes. Or have the defender overplay one of the offensive players.

- Limit the number of passes or time the offense has to get in position and take a shot. Reduce the number of ball touches for a person's possession.

- Place the coach in as a second defender. If necessary, restrict the second defender initially (e.g., the defender becomes active only after a certain number of passes).

- Allow the second defender to stand outside the playing area and become a defender after a specified number of passes.

- Try 2-on-2 or 3-on-2 for a short time and evaluate play.

TEACHABLE MOMENT

When players move well to get open and receive passes, the team-mates get a good feeling. This encourages good passing and cooperation. Reinforce this by pinpointing when appropriate. Discuss how professional teams must work together like this, too.

Chapter 10

Learning Experiences for Fielding Games

Fielding games include some or all of the following: running, batting or striking, throwing and catching, and kicking. All the games in this category involve fielding. There is overlap with other categories, but when fielding is a major emphasis, the game is included in the fielding category. Fielding games require considerable space, usually outdoors. Children need a high degree of self-responsibility to work in separate games of this complexity. The parent fielding games, if used, demand many sophisticated skills and strategies, which are difficult to learn and execute without extensive practice. This makes fielding games difficult to plan, organize, and supervise. The four learning experiences given in this category help children develop skills that transfer to other fielding games.

Focus	Name	Suggested grade range
Repositioning, passing, and avoiding being caught	Runner, Stay Away	3-4
Catching and throwing	Bounce and Field	4-6
Fielding batted fly and ground balls	300	4-6
Batting and fielding	Strategy Fielding	5-6

RUNNER, STAY AWAY*

Prerequisites

- Experience in Trio Keep-Away (chapter 9)
- Practice in receiving balls from several directions, with many types of arcs and speeds
- Practice using a quick release (holding the ball for a brief time) to pass to a partner

Objectives

As a result of participating in this learning experience, students will improve their ability to

- Use speed and direction changes that mislead or confuse opposing players anticipating one's pathway
- Use crisp, quick-release passes to move a ball ahead of a runner
- Reposition themselves in relation to the runner and teammates (3-4, #20)

Suggested Grade Range

Intermediate (3-4)

Organization

Groups of 4 children move anywhere within an area at least 20 feet × 30 feet; a team of 3 has the ball, and a 4th person must stay away from the ball.

Equipment Needed

1 8-inch ball (rubber, plastic, or foam) per group of 4; cones, lines, or markers to set boundaries (which can be changed as the group and teacher decide)

Description

"This is a fun, quick game I think you'll like. It's called Runner, Stay Away. The game uses a group of 4—1 runner and 3 fielders. In an area about as large as within the cones you see, the 3 fielders must keep the ball moving with little or no holding. They pass the ball in relation to where the runner is moving so they can gently tag the runner with the ball. The runner tries to stay away from the ball by dodging and changing directions quickly, based on what the team of 3 does with the ball. The runner can move anywhere in the space, sometimes close to people, sometimes away from them, but attempts to stay as far from the ball as possible so he or she doesn't get tagged.

"If you're a fielder, you'll need to move when you do *not* have the ball to figure out where the runner may go. It will be hard to do. If the runner is tagged, the runner and 1 of the fielders exchange roles. Or do this after six passes [or any number challenging to the group]. When I say 'Go,' get your groups of 4 and your ball, decide who will be the runner first, and set up your cones and begin. Go! [During practice, give remaining directions.] Remember, the 3 fielders must reposition themselves in relation to the runner and the ball. The idea is to cover the entire area around the runner and pass the ball close to the runner. Good! I see you're moving and watching what your partners are doing."

*Note. From *Physical Education for Children: A Focus on the Teaching Process* by B.J. Logson, N.R. Barrett, M. Ammons, M.R. Broer, L.E. Halverson, R. McGee, and M.A. Robertson, 1984, Philadelphia: Lea & Febiger. Copyright 1984 by B.J. Logson. Adapted by permission of B.J. Logson.

Look For

- Children making quick and accurate decisions about where to pass and to whom; children planning the pass or anticipating where teammates will be moving.
- Passers holding the ball a short time to make appropriate decisions.
- Repositioning for advantage after passing or after a runner moves past what formerly was a good position.
- Varied strategy on the part of the runners.

How Can I Change This?

- Increase the area size to aid the runner or decrease the area size to aid the fielders.
- Add a 4th person to help the fielders.
- If tagging the runner is too difficult, the fielders may throw the ball to hit the runner below the waist.
- Use a considerably longer and narrower playing area so that the runner has to get from a starting line to a goal line.
- Have 5 or 6 fielders try to prevent a runner from moving through the area, touching a base, and returning across the starting line. When skill permits, position 5 or 6 children at the starting line. When a runner is tagged or successfully returns to the starting line, another runner begins running immediately. This keeps the action continuous. The fielders must adjust quickly to focus on subsequent runners. (See Figure 10.1.)

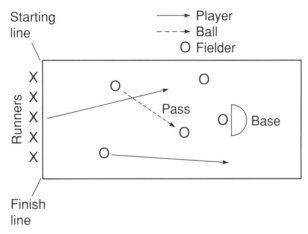

Figure 10.1   Extended version of Runner, Stay Away.

TEACHABLE MOMENT

Discuss how talking with teammates can help or not. How does it help? How does it make it harder?

BOUNCE AND FIELD

Prerequisites

- Practice throwing a ball that hits the floor, then a wall, and then rebounds into the air away from the wall
- Success in catching bouncing and aerial balls thrown with medium force

Objectives

As a result of participating in this learning experience, children will improve their ability to

- Adjust bounce-throws so that the ball lands in the target area (5-6, #1)
- Position and move to conceal where one will go and to decide the best position to field the bounced ball (5-6, #24)

Suggested Grade Range

Intermediate (4-6)

Organization

One child is positioned anywhere in the fielding area; another child, the thrower, may position anywhere in the throwing area. A 10-foot wide area that extends from the wall on one side of the gymnasium to the wall on the other side is needed.

Equipment Needed

1 ball per pair (small rubber ball or tennis ball); cones, lines, or tape. Outside, a wall or pitchbacks could be used (see Figure 10.2).

Figure 10.2   Bounce and Field.

Description

"Our game today really requires good thinkers! It requires you to decide the direction, arc, and force of throwing a ball that will bounce on the floor [or ground], hit a wall, and then get sent into a playing area. Let's watch one time and see if Jones, the thrower, can make the ball bounce into the area marked by the cones.

[Explain during demonstration.] "He has to stand anywhere between the tape line [or other boundary] and the wall and throw the ball so it bounces on the floor, then on the wall target, and then into the cone target area on the floor. Yes, Jones can do that. Now, we'll add Katie as a fielder. [Students demonstrate.] When the ball goes past the first cone [or line], Katie tries to catch the ball in as few bounces as possible, preferably on a fly ball. Jones gets 1 point for each bounce *after* the ball passes the first cone [or line]. So, the throwers want a lot of bounces but the fielder tries not to let it bounce. After five throws, switch roles. When I say 'Go,' get into pairs, pick one of the long, narrow playing areas already marked off, choose starting roles, and begin play. Go!

[After play begins and if necessary.] "Throwers, you may have only three fakes before you send the ball. [Or limit to 4 seconds after the fielder indicates he or she is ready to play.] Stop. Fielders, decide where you need to stand to be in the best position to catch and field each ball. Throwers, vary where you send the ball depending on where the fielder is positioned. Change where you stand in the batting or sending area, and how you angle the ball on the floor and wall. Fielders, you may want to vary your starting positions in the field, even faking and changing positions as the batter throws. Keep these ideas in mind and begin again. Go."

Look for

- Throwers varying the ball flight by changing where they bounce the ball on the floor and on the wall.
- Fielders varying and changing starting positions but still being ready to move in other directions in case their prediction is inaccurate.

How Can I Change This?

- To make this easier for the thrower, make the playing area wider *or* move the first line closer to the wall.
- To make this easier for the fielder, make the playing area narrower or shorter, or move the first line (line the ball must cross) further from the wall.
- Use 2 fielders, 1 by the first line and the other deeper. Have fielders throw to a target after fielding the ball.
- Use traditional softball scoring—one bounce catch is a single, two bounces a double, and so on—and after three outs, change players' roles. A ball that bounces before the first cone (or line) and is caught is an out.

300

Prerequisites

- Success in moving to catch a variety of ground, bouncing, and aerial balls
- Ability to self-toss and hit a ball at least half the time

Objectives

As a result of participating in this learning experience, children will improve their ability to

- Place-hit balls within an area
- Position to catch or field a variety of balls (3-4, #20)
- Call for the ball when it is nearest to them and be considerate of others when calling and catching (3-4, #27)

Suggested Grade Range

Intermediate (4-6)

Organization

One batter faces 2 to 4 fielders in a V-shaped area 50 feet long and 30 to 50 feet wide at the end of the V (see Figure 10.3).

Equipment Needed

1 plastic bat and 5 to 10 Wiffle balls for each group; 1 large poster showing how to score points. (If needed, a batting tee for some groups, and perhaps small foam balls.)

Description

"Your parents may remember this game, so it's been around a long time. One of you is the batter, and the others in the group will field the balls. Fielders, you are trying to earn enough points, 300, to get the batter *out* and allow a new person to bat. Here's

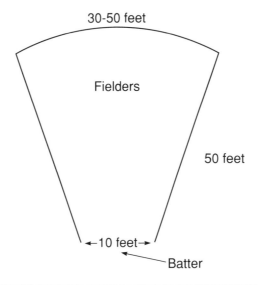

Figure 10.3   300 playing area.

how you can earn points. [Show poster with point totals and categories.] You get 25 points for catching a grounder or a ball on three or more bounces; 50 points for catching a ball on two bounces; 75 points for catching a ball on only one bounce; and 100 points for catching a ball on a fly (no bounces).

"Here's the idea. You add up the points you make from catching. You want to be the first in your group to get to 300 points. When you do that, the batter is out and you get to bat. If you miss a ball, you lose the number of points the ball was worth. So, if you missed a fly ball, how many points do you lose? That's right. 100. Get the idea? You may take chances to score more points, but be careful not to miss, either. I will keep this poster up as you play so you can look at it when you need to.

"Fielders, you need to say 'Mine' when the ball is nearest to you, to tell the other players it is your chance. You shouldn't be trying to catch balls in other people's spaces. Batters, try to hit all kinds of balls and hit to all the players by following through to your target. You can use a tee to bat or toss it to yourself.

"When I say 'Go,' you need to get into groups of 3 [or 4 or 5, depending on the number of fielders]. Move to one of the fields already set up and begin to play. [Each field has several plastic bats and 5 to 10 Wiffle balls.] Quickly, how many points do you need before a batter is out? Yes, 300. Go!

[During practice.] "Batters, remember to give yourself easy tosses that come straight down so that you need to reach to hit the ball. Fielders, remember to call for your catches. Felicia's group is doing that very well.

"I notice that one group wants to change the rules a little and say that 1 person can't bat for more than 5 minutes at a time, in case it's taking a long time for the fielders to get to 300 points. That's OK, as long as your whole group agrees on the change. Steve's group decided to have everyone bat before anyone could bat a second time. That's a good idea."

Look For

- Fielders concentrating, calling for balls in their area, and aligning to catch the balls.
- Batters trying to place balls in different areas of the field.

How Can I Change This?

- Use a smaller field or lighter, softer ball to help the fielders.
- Have a partner help the batter by giving an easy setup toss.
- Have players catch punted or kicked balls; this may be easier and will accomplish similar objectives. You can also use Frisbees or other objects.
- Use a larger field, a wooden bat, and a safety baseball.
- After a successful field, have the fielder throw to a catcher stationed to the side and safely away from the batter.
- Change to 400 or 500 points if needed because of fielding skill.

STRATEGY FIELDING*

Prerequisites

- Practice positioning and fielding thrown and batted balls that require fielders to move in order to catch
- Skill in hitting a setup toss from a partner

Objectives

As a result of participating in this learning experience, children will improve their ability to

- Place-hit a ball set up by a partner
- Cooperate and communicate to position themselves to field based on a predetermined strategy

Suggested Grade Range

Intermediate (5-6)

Organization

One batter is near home plate with a partner who is 3 to 6 feet to the side with a ball. Two fielders are positioned anywhere within a fielding area at least 12 feet by 24 feet (but preferably larger). There is a distance of 24 feet from the batter to the fielding area (modify this depending on hitting and fielding abilities). See Figure 10.4.

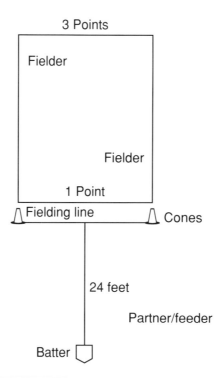

Figure 10.4   Strategy Fielding.

*Note. From *Rethinking Games Teaching* (pp. 32-33) by R. Thorpe, D. Bunker, and L. Almond, 1986, Irthingborough, Northants, England: Nene Litho. Copyright 1986 by University of Technology. Adapted by permission.

Equipment Needed

1 rubber base, 1 plastic bat, and 1 Wiffle ball (or foam ball) per group; cones, markers, or lines for the fielding area; 1 big diagram of Figure 10.4.

Description

"Today we're going to play a fun game called Strategy Fielding. It's played with 4 players—2 on the batting team and 2 on the fielding team. In Strategy Fielding the player with the ball needs to toss a very good pitch or setup to the batter. We've practiced this before. In today's game, the batter gets three pitches to hit the ball through the fielding area, but below head level. It would be easy if we didn't have that rule. The batting team—the batter and pitcher—scores 1 point if the ball passes the first set of cones and 3 points if the ball passes the back boundary line. After the partners on the batting team both have had 3 at-bats, the fielding team gets to bat. Fielders, you are trying to keep the ball from going very far. You can play anywhere inside the playing area and can even play slightly in front of the 1-point cones. See the fielding line where Jill is standing? Or you can play back near the 3-point line, where Jill is now. [Jill moves.] Or anywhere in between. You have to do a lot of planning to figure out where you should stand.

"On 'Go,' get into groups of 4, then get equipment—each group needs 1 rubber base, 1 plastic bat, and 1 Wiffle ball, plus cones for markers. Set up as in the big diagram here, decide who does what, plan your strategy, and begin play. Go. [If the children set up the play areas and then decide partners and strategy, there could be a relatively lengthy time before the games begin. Teachers may want to set up ahead of time to save time. Children do, however, need time to plan how to defend and hit, especially with a new game like this.]

[After some play.] "Stop. Fielders, what positioning seems to work best for your team? Have you stayed with one strategy, or have you tried different ones? Pitchers, can you change the type of pitch you give your partner, depending on the type of hit you both have planned? Have you discussed this? Do you need to?

"Pitchers, you may also want to adjust where you stand and how you set up the ball for your partner. What can the person who pitches the ball do to help what the batter intends to do? [Adjust the throw so that it drops as much vertically as possible to make it easy for the batter.] OK, with this in mind, let's begin again. Go."

Look For

- Partners cooperating with one another in planning and executing batting and fielding strategies.
- Fielders working together to apply strategies they both know.

How Can I Change This?

- No changes are suggested. Any changes should develop in individual games and be accepted by those involved.
- This game could also be used with kicking and possibly throwing.

> **TEACHABLE MOMENT**
>
> Discuss what type of positioning strategy for fielding results in the fewest points being scored, both at individual games and with the whole class.

Appendix

All of us are concerned about the time it takes to plan and write lessons, and many of us, especially beginning teachers, have difficulty with such planning. Besides providing direction for actual teaching, lesson plans are written records (often now stored on computer disks) that can be useful for future instructional and accountability records. Lesson plans are especially important for beginning teachers, and also for experienced teachers when they are teaching new content. The following includes components of a lesson plan and one extended lesson.

Lesson Plan Components

Lesson plans need to focus on the following components. (Many of these can be planned mentally by experienced teachers.)

Date(s) _____ *Class / Grade* _____
Main lesson focus
Lesson #___ of ___ total lessons in the unit
Readiness (background information about students)
Objectives
  For students
  For the teacher
Equipment needed
Organization of equipment and students
Plan to begin the lesson

Sequence of content (includes teaching cues for feedback and observation purposes)
Safety, if applicable
Plan to close the lesson (if used)
References (if needed to remember it)
Evaluation
  Student learning (most important)
  Management
  Teaching behaviors

Lesson planning can take many forms. I am wary of suggesting any specific form because of the amount of space for each component. Preservice teachers feel that they have to *fill* the space allotted even if they don't need to and that they can't use *more* if they need to. I would prefer teachers to plan using a form that fits them.

Although most formal instruction asks teachers to decide on objectives first, many teachers thoroughly plan their activities first. If you work this way, that's fine. I have found that preservice physical educators have the most difficulty sequencing activities, writing down the main points they wish to emphasize, and developing extensions (Rink, 1985) to make that one activity easier or harder for students. For a skill lesson (games Stage 2), listing refinement ideas is essential. For competitive game lessons, extensions and strategies to be used are very important.

Sample Lesson Plan

Date(s)   March 4 to 6   *Class/Grade*   all fourths

Main lesson focus   Invasion game, Hoop Guard

Lesson #   1 of 3 total lessons in the unit.

Readiness   Students have experience in throwing beanbags to targets and in balancing so they can move in many directions, including moving to catch objects.

Student objectives   Faking and quick release of a beanbag toward a hoop guarded by another person; defending by using body and hands to shield the goal from throws. See the activity description for Hoop Guard in chapter 9.

Teacher objectives   I will watch for students who need extra help in using the body to block an object and those who need or could use ideas for varying their strategies.
- Ask questions that make children think about strategies.
- Emphasize both faking and reading fakes.
- Observe by scanning all small-group play.
- Make modification suggestions depending on abilities at individual games.

Equipment needed   1 beanbag or foam object and 1 hoop for each set of partners.

Organization of equipment and students   Pairs will position themselves away from others in a 10-foot by 35-foot space. Students select partners of similar ability or make equitable games with changes, such as with differing restraining lines.

Plan to begin the lesson   In scattered space children will practice moving, including running, to avoid others. Then I'll call them in closer to show another child and me playing Hoop Guard. After the children understand, I'll have them set up the equipment and begin play.

Sequence of content

Learning piece	Strategy focus	Observation focus	Ways to extend
1a. Offensive faking, moving to get a high-percentage throw at hoop target	Moving, faking	Variety in fakes, moving defender high/low, side to side	Easier Larger target, move line in Harder Smaller target, set time limit
1b. Defender using body to guard or block shot attempts	Wide shape in direction of throw, reading throw, using arms and legs to block	Body shape, legs and arms in relation to beanbag and throw; balance; good sideward movement	Easier Use a small plastic bottle inside the hoop as the target Harder Guard 2 or 3 hoops positioned next to each other
2. After a shot or score, either player may obtain the beanbag and continue play.	Quick transitions as play continues	Avoiding contact but moving to retrieve the beanbag	
3. Restraining line changed to a circle 3 feet to 5 feet outside the hoop	Fakes and side moves	Faking and good sideward movement	A nonthrower assistant for the offense

Safety   Safety between groups, especially sideways. Switch to foam balls if beanbags present a safety problem.

To close the lesson, I will

Emphasize offensive and defensive strategies that were
- Used consistently by many children
- Used and resulted in many successful shots or blocked shots
- Different as a result of extensions in the game

Reference   Doolittle & Girard (1991) in *JOPERD*.

Evaluation

For students, this will accomplish
- Faking and then quick throwing to aim at a guarded target
- Positioning one's body shape in relation to beanbag position and in relation to the goal and throw direction to reduce opponent's chances of scoring
- Using one's hands and body parts to catch, block throws
- Learning to make transition after a throw or score to keep the game going

Teaching behaviors
- Have children answer questions about strategies used and why.
- Did I emphasize both faking and reading fakes?
- Did I observe by scanning all small-group play?
- Did I make modification suggestions depending on abilities at individual games?

Evaluation of learning
- Record the strategies used most, with most success. Compare this list with subsequent performance.
- Record major problems and successes on offense and defense.
- If possible, videotape 3 to 5 minutes of play for instructor evaluations and for class viewing after 1 or 2 subsequent lessons.

So Where Do We Go From Here?

We hope that reading this book has left you full of thoughts, some questions, and most of all, *excitement* about teaching this content area. We hope it makes you eager to get out there and try some of the ideas and learning experiences with your children . . . to take a closer look at your curriculum . . . to maybe give you that "something extra" you needed in order to take another try at teaching this content to your children.

And although we know that implementing many of the ideas in this book with your children probably won't be quite as easy as it was to read about them, we hope that this book goes a long way in helping you to get there. We hope that it encourages you to talk with other teachers, ask questions, and search for solutions that will make your teaching, and your students' learning experiences, the best they can be!

We here in the Child Health Division of Human Kinetics Publishers want you to know that you're not out there alone in your quest to improve your teaching and the physical education experiences of your students. We do our best to provide you with current information and professional support through our many programs and resources. Examples of these include our American Master Teacher Program for Children's Physical Education (AMTP), which this book is a part of; the national newsletter *Teaching Elementary Physical Education* (*TEPE*); the annual national Conference on Teaching Elementary Physical Education, which we cosponsor; and our outcomes-based student and teacher resources.

Many of you have written or called us in the past with a neat idea you wanted to share with others in *TEPE*, a question on where to find some information, or even just to say thanks for a job well done. We hope that you'll continue to let us know what your questions, concerns, and thoughts are and how we can help you even better in the future. Feel free to write us at P.O. Box 5076, Champaign, IL 61825-5076, or call us at 1-800-747-4457. We'll do our best to help you out!

Until then,

The staff of the Child Health Division of Human Kinetics

References

Belka, D.E. (1978). Teaching is like coaching. *Future Focus*, **1**(1), 10-11.

Belka, D.E. (1985). Effects of selected sequencing factors on the catching process of elementary school children. *Journal of Teaching in Physical Education*, **5**, 42-51.

Belka, D.E. (1990). Learning to be a games player. *Strategies*, **44**(4), 8-10.

Buschner, C. (1994). *Teaching children movement concepts and skills: Becoming a master teacher*. Champaign, IL: Human Kinetics.

Council on Physical Education for Children. (1992). *Developmentally appropriate physical education practices for children*. Reston, VA: National Association for Sport and Physical Education.

Doolittle, S. (1992, May 1). *Teaching children to understand games*. Paper presented at East Coast Regional Games Conference, Hofstra University, Long Island, NY.

Doolittle, S., & Girard, K.T. (1991). A dynamic approach to teaching games in elementary PE. *Journal of Physical Education, Recreation and Dance*, **62**(4), 57-63.

Earls, R. (1985). *Developmental games stages*. Unpublished manuscript, State Department of South Carolina, Columbia, SC.

Figley, G.E., Mitchell, H.C., & Wright, B.L. (1986). *Elementary physical education: An educational experience* (2nd ed.). Dubuque, IA: Kendall/Hunt.

Franck, M., Graham, G., Lawson, H., Loughrey, T., Ritson, R., Sanborn, M., & Seefeldt, V. (1991). *Physical education outcomes: A project of the National Association for Sport and Physical Education*. Reston, VA: National Association for Sport and Physical Education.

Graham, G. (1992). *Teaching children physical education: Becoming a master teacher*. Champaign, IL: Human Kinetics.

Graham, G., Holt/Hale, S., & Parker, M. (1993). *Children moving* (3rd ed.). Mountain View, CA: Mayfield.

Griffin, P.S. (1981). One small step for personkind: Observations and suggestions for sex equity in coeducational physical education classes. *Journal of Teaching in Physical Education*, Introductory issue, 4-12.

Herkowitz, J. (1978). Developmental task analysis: The design of movement experiences and evaluation of motor development status. In M. Ridenour (Ed.), *Motor development issues and applications* (pp. 139-164). Princeton, NJ: Princeton Book Company.

Kelly, L.E. (1989). Instructional time: The overlooked factor in PE curriculum development. *Journal of Physical Education, Recreation and Dance*, **60**(6), 29-32.

Logsdon, B.J., Barrett, K.R., Ammons, M., Broer, M.R., Halverson, L.E., McGee, R., & Roberton, M.A. (1984). *Physical education for children: A focus on the teaching process*. Philadelphia: Lea & Febiger.

Luxbacher, J.A. (1991). *Teaching soccer: Steps to success*. Champaign, IL: Leisure Press.

Melograno, V. (1979). *Designing curriculum and learning: A physical education coeducational approach*. Dubuque, IA: Kendall/Hunt.

Morris, G.S.D. (1976). *How to change the games children play*. Minneapolis: Burgess.

Morris, G.S.D. (1980). *How to change the games children play* (2nd ed.). Minneapolis: Burgess.

Morris, G.S.D., & Stiehl, J. (1989). *Changing kids' games*. Champaign, IL: Human Kinetics.

Pottak, K. (1992, April 30). *Student created games in 5th and 6th grade*. Paper presented at East Coast Regional Games Conference, Hofstra University, Long Island, NY.

Purcell, T. (1994). *Teaching children dance: Becoming a master teacher*. Champaign, IL: Human Kinetics.

Ratliffe, T., & Ratliffe, L. (1994). *Teaching children fitness: Becoming a master teacher.* Champaign, IL: Human Kinetics.

Redden, W.L. (1992). Confederates: A system that works. *Strategies,* **5**(5), 12-15.

Riley, M. (1975). Games and humanism. *Journal of Physical Education and Recreation,* **46**(2), 46-49.

Rink, J.E. (1985). *Teaching physical education for learning.* St. Louis: Times Mirror/Mosby.

Rink, J.E. (1992). *Teaching physical education for learning* (2nd ed.). St. Louis: Times Mirror/Mosby.

Roberton, M.A., & Halverson, L.A. (1984). *Developing children: Their changing movement.* Philadelphia: Lea & Febiger.

Romance, T.J. (1985). Observing for confidence. *Journal of Physical Education, Recreation and Dance,* **56**(6), 47-49.

Schwager, S. (1992). Relay races: Are they appropriate for elementary physical education? *Journal of Physical Education, Recreation and Dance,* **63**(6), 54-56.

Siedentop, D. (1991). *Developing teaching skills in physical education* (3rd ed.). Mountain View, CA: Mayfield.

Thorpe, R., Bunker, D., & Almond, L. (1986). *Rethinking games teaching.* Irthingborough, Northants, England: Nene Litho.

Werner, P. (1994). *Teaching children gymnastics: Becoming a master teacher.* Champaign, IL: Human Kinetics.

Werner, P., & Almond, L. (1990). Models of games education. *Journal of Physical Education, Recreation and Dance,* **61**(4), 23-27.

Wikgren, S. (1992). Fitness: What's the right approach for children? *Teaching Elementary Physical Education,* **4**(1), 1, 6-7.

Williams, H.G. (1983). *Perceptual and motor development.* Englewood Cliffs, NJ: Prentice Hall.

Williams, N.F. (1992). The physical education hall of shame. *Journal of Physical Education, Recreation and Dance,* **63**(6), 57-60.

Wilson, N.S. (1976). *The frequency and patterns of utilization of selected motor skills by third and fourth grade girls and boys in the game of kickball.* Unpublished master's project, University of Georgia, Athens.

Suggested Readings

Books and articles included in this annotated bibliography contain ideas and information that can be used to evaluate or change one's program. The entries were selected because they contain (a) overall high quality, (b) very useful ideas even though overall quality contained some weak aspects, or (c) recent developments or approaches to teaching games.

Ballou, P.B. (1982). *Teaching beginning badminton*. Minneapolis: Burgess.

Most of this book is designed for beginning instruction of secondary or older learners. Ideas on 2-person coverage (p. 68) and strategy concepts (p. 77) and, especially, an analysis of situation and shot selection (p. 121) are very useful.

Belka, D.E. (1990). Learning to be a games player. *Strategies*, **4**(4), 8-10.

This article builds on Judy Rink's ideas for Stage 3 game playing using basketball as an extended example. The games stages are related to motor learning, and prerequisites are listed. A progression series and questions to ask when introducing beginning offensive and defensive strategies are explained.

Doolittle, S.A., & Girard, K.T. (1991). A dynamic approach to teaching games in elementary PE. *Journal of Physical Education, Recreation and Dance*, **62**(4), 57-62.

The authors advocate a problem-solving approach that emphasizes basic concepts and strategies of games rather than mainly skill acquisition. The authors describe a game sequence using hoops and beanbags to teach basic scoring concepts as well as goalkeeper strategies. The concepts emphasized are then related to floor hockey to show transfer of strategies to another type of invasion game.

Figley, G.E., Mitchell, H.C., & Wright, B.L. (1986). *Elementary school physical education: An educational experience* (2nd ed.). Dubuque, IA: Kendall/Hunt.

Chapter 3, simply titled "Games," clearly explains guidelines for analyzing and revising games for children. Several examples describe games that are not worthy of inclusion in programs, ones that can be revised to be acceptable, and ones that are worthy without revision. Much useful information is included, especially about specific objectives in psychomotor, cognitive, and affective domains. In addition, three overlapping but progressive phases of games address sequence in games instruction. A major flaw is the lack of development of strategy or understanding about quality of game play.

Graham, G., Holt/Hale, S., & Parker, M. (1993). *Children moving: A teacher's guide to developing a successful physical education program* (3rd ed.). Mountain View, CA: Mayfield.

Content in elementary physical education is determined by combining skill themes and movement concepts. Skill themes are basic motor patterns that are used in games, gymnastics, and dance. Movement concepts are ideas that help one move better and understand why one is moving better. Many movement concepts are based on the Laban framework. Constant throughout the book is the development of content ideas based on a model that categorizes skill proficiency into four levels. Each level has developmental characteristics that can be applied to any of the movement skill themes. The 11 skill theme chapters include ones on traveling, jumping and landing, rolling, balancing, throwing and catching, and striking with long-handled implements. In each chapter, activities are described for each of the four proficiency levels. There are chapters on teaching dance, gymnastics, and games as well as on physical fitness and mainstreaming. There are more activities with clearer directions for teaching single and combination skills than for teaching beginning offensive and defensive game playing.

Human Kinetics Publishers. (in press). *Teaching for outcomes in elementary physical education: A guide for curriculum and assessment.* Human Kinetics: Champaign, IL.

This unique resource is divided into two parts. Part I introduces the concept of purposeful planning (creating curriculum goals or outcomes that are realistic and achievable for your particular situation) and then shows how to assess these goals using portfolio and performance task assessments. Teachers will find the many practical hints helpful, especially concerning the use and scoring of these assessments. Part II is organized according to the concepts (including fitness concepts) and skills taught in physical education and provides sample performance and portfolio tasks; teachers can use many of these to directly assess NASPE "Benchmarks," which are referenced when applicable. The "learnable pieces" are detailed for each skill and concept, along with activity ideas and practical hints for teaching them at the varying grade levels.

Logsdon, B.J., Alleman, L.M., Clark, D., & Parent Sakola, S. (1986). *Physical education teaching units for program development Grades K-3.* Philadelphia: Lea & Febiger.

This book includes detailed and useful unit plans for 32 game units for Grades K-3 along with units for gymnastics and dance. Each unit is a guide, not a lesson plan, for building three to eight lessons about that particular unit focus. Laban's framework is present in each resource plan. Student objectives, equipment needs, and learning tasks are described very clearly. Games units stress single and combination skills learning and quality performance.

Logsdon, B.J., Alleman, L.M., Clark, D., & Parent Sakola, S. (1986). *Physical education teaching units for program development Grades 4-6.* Philadelphia: Lea & Febiger.

A similar format is used by these same authors for 22 resource game unit plans for Grades 4, 5, and 6. A summary chart shows all units in games, gymnastics, and dance. In fourth grade, the emphasis is on throwing lead passes, using empty space, and repositioning before and after receiving or sending an object. Three of the seven units in fourth grade involve learning offensive and defensive game strategies. Six of the eight units in fifth grade focus on game strategies, and net work in the other two units emphasizes combination skill practice. All of the sixth-grade units include competitive game play with specific emphases, such as cutting off passing lanes, backing up throws, and repositioning.

Logsdon, B.J., Barrett, K.R., Ammons, M., Broer, M.R., Halverson, L.E., McGee, R., & Roberton, M.A. (1984). *Physical education for children: A focus on the teaching process* (2nd ed.). Philadelphia: Lea & Febiger.

Now out of print, this book has excellent chapters on motor development and on mechanical principles applied to basic movement skills. Chapter 5 presents educational games information and includes a number of clear examples. Later chapters cover observation skills and also evaluation of processes and products, many for single and combination skills. The book is repetitive but not redundant, and that is one of its strengths.

McGee, R., & Farrow, A. (1987). *Test questions for physical education activities.* Champaign, IL: Human Kinetics.

Complete written knowledge tests for 12 game-related activities are available. A section of each test contains questions on strategy, in addition to six other topics. All test questions are multiple-choice.

McGettigan, J.P. (1987). *Soccer drills for individual and team play* (pp. 102-104). West Nyack, NY: Parker.

A list of factors goalkeepers must know when defending is listed on page 102. Good ideas about narrowing the shooting angle by moving out under control to meet unprotected shooting attempts are explained on pages 103 to 104.

Morris, G.S.D. (1976). *How to change the games children play.* Minneapolis: Burgess.

This easy-to-read book presents roles that games achieve, a model for analyzing games, and use of this model for student decision making. The premise is to think about games and use the model to change how teachers design games for children and how children design and understand games. Teachers can modify aspects of movement skills for observation and assessment, even for individualizing motor skill instruction. The games examples depart from traditional concepts of what games are. Some of the examples, useful in 1976, are no longer appropriate.

Morris, G.S.D. (1980). *How to change the games children play* (2nd ed.). Minneapolis: Burgess.

This edition is similar to the first edition. Both concentrate on including all children in games and helping children experience emotionally positive, social activities. Activity examples develop these ideas.

Morris, G.S.D., & Stiehl, J. (1989). *Changing kids' games*. Champaign, IL: Human Kinetics.

This book contains many ideas for analyzing and designing games. Like earlier versions of *How to Change the Games Children Play* (Morris, 1976, 1980), this easy-to-read book has many ideas to accommodate individual differences in games, change games to make children feel comfortable, and modify activities from a motor development perspective. Morris's 1989 update, published with co-author Jim Stiehl, adds evaluation tools for self-confidence, interests, and player attitudes. The games examples in all three books are not at the quality level of the conceptual ideas and frameworks presented. In fact, many examples include significant waiting time and may not be appropriate for building game strategy and developing good games players. The conceptual ideas and ways to modify games make this a valuable book.

Peterson, S.C. (1992). The sequence of instruction in games: Implication for developmental appropriateness. *Journal of Physical Education, Recreation and Dance*, **63**(6), 36 39.

This article is part of a special feature on developmentally appropriate physical education for children in this issue. Four major guidelines were explained for teachers to consider when sequencing learning experiences for children's games. Peterson ties sequence to (a) children's motor development, (b) using problem solving and differentiated

tasks to individualize instruction, (c) ideas for gradual increases in complexity of tasks, and (d) relationships of lesson parts to each other, lessons to subsequent lessons, and even years to subsequent years.

Phillip, J.A., & Wilkerson, J.D. (1990). *Teaching team sports: A coeducational approach*. Champaign, IL: Human Kinetics.

This book provides information, explanations, and concept definitions for introducing team sports, planning practices and drills, and understanding movement observation and motor learning. High-quality analyses of skill progressions and error detection and correction are given with less emphasis on strategy. Separate chapters are organized for basketball, field hockey, touch football, soccer, softball, speedball, and volleyball.

Robson, B. (1987). *Bryan Robson's SOCCER Drills*. New York: Sterling.

This book has many drills, most of which are too difficult for beginners. A few portions of the book emphasize tactics or strategy. These are explained clearly, and good diagrams make these strategy explanations useful, even for beginners.

Southworth, S.H. (1989). *High percentage base running*. Champaign, IL: Human Kinetics.

Devoted exclusively to base running, this book includes many advanced concepts. Diagrams and explanations can be useful when planning base-running games. If small-group play is designed for 1, 2, or 3 runners on base and a batter is pitched to, this book can be a valuable resource.

Spindt, G.B., Weinberg, H., Hennessy, B., Holyoak, C., & Monti, W. (1993). *Moving as a team: Middle school physical education* (teacher's ed.). Dubuque, IA: Kendall/Hunt.

This is one of three textbooks designed for instruction in middle school physical education. The book is designed to provide children, ages 10 to 14, with a self-study in physical education, as well as participation with others in cooperative and competitive activities. Chapters on physical fitness, communication through sports, and self-image help this self-study. Developmental changes, gender issues, and multicultural considerations are also included. This book's strong points include easy reading, excellent organization, many pictures, and game strategy ideas.

Thorpe, R., Bunker, D., & Almond, L. (1986). *Rethinking games teaching*. Irthingborough, Northants, England: Nene Litho.

The basic premise is that games teaching needs to focus on the contextual nature of the game rather than on specific skills. Understanding strategy and the nature of the game will enable learners to see a need for skill and technique. The traditional emphasis is on skill performance, which is often unrelated to understanding how to play the game. *Why* needs to be understood before *how*. Several models, examples, and discussions help readers understand games and even categories of games.

Viera, B.L., & Ferguson, B.J. (1989). *Teaching volleyball: Steps to success*. Champaign, IL: Leisure Press.

The book focuses on teaching volleyball skills. Although this book is intended for secondary or higher instruction, it includes many good ideas that elementary school teachers can use, as do other books in this series. Ideas about play in real game situations (pp. 226-229), game play choices (pp. 230-231), and self-evaluating one's play (pp. 232-233) may be useful in planning and teaching volleyball to beginners. A companion book (*Volleyball: Steps to success*) focuses on skills and progressions of skills.

Werner, P., & Almond, L. (1990). Models of games education. *Journal of Physical Education, Recreation and Dance*, **61**(4), 23-27.

This is an explanation and comparison of three models of games education, including the Thorpe, Bunker, and Almond classification. It is more available and easier to understand than the 1986 book by these three authors.

About the Author

David Belka, an associate professor of teacher education at Miami University in Oxford, Ohio, has a wealth of experience in developing and teaching games. For 9 years he taught games as part of elementary physical education and intramural curricula in New Castle, Pennsylvania, and Toledo, Ohio. His research on children's perceptual-motor functioning and catching skills, more than a decade of teaching games progressions in undergraduate courses, professional publications, and experience in conducting in-service teacher workshops enabled him to create the developmental approach he applies to the games in this book.

David Belka earned his PhD in elementary physical education from the University of Toledo in 1976. He is a member of the American Alliance for Health, Physical Education, Recreation and Dance and actively contributes to the field of elementary physical education by presenting papers and poster board sessions, planning symposia, and reviewing articles.

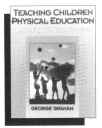

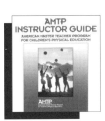

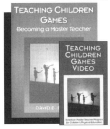